FASHIONISTO

A CENTURY OF
STYLE ICONS

SIMONE WERLE

FASHIONISTO

A CENTURY OF
STYLE ICONS

3 1336 08531 6090

PRESTEL

MUNICH | BERLIN | LONDON | NEW YORK

© Prestel, Munich · Berlin · London · New York 2010

Front cover: James Dean
Back cover: Oscar Wilde, Johnny Depp, John Galliano,
Boy George; large image: Frank Sinatra
Frontispiece: Mick Jagger

Picture credits: see page 172

Prestel would like to thank

 gettyimages® and

for their kind cooperation

Prestel Verlag, Munich
A member of Verlagsgruppe Random House GmbH

Prestel Verlag
Königinstrasse 9
80539 Munich
Tel. +49 (0)89 24 29 08-300
Fax +49 (0)89 24 29 08-335

Prestel Publishing Ltd.
4 Bloomsbury Place
London WC1A 2QA
Tel. +44 (0)20 7323-5004
Fax +44 (0)20 7636-8004

Prestel Publishing
900 Broadway, Suite 603
New York, NY 10003
Tel. +1 (212) 995-2720
Fax +1 (212) 995-2733

www.prestel.com

Library of Congress Control Number: 2010933776

British Library Cataloguing-in-Publication Data: a catalogue
record for this book is available from the British Library;
Deutsche Nationalbibliothek holds a record of this publication
in the Deutsche Nationalbibliografie; detailed bibliographical
data can be found under: http://dnb.d-nb.de

Prestel books are available worldwide. Please contact
your nearest bookseller or one of the above addresses for
information concerning your local distributor.

Translated from the German by Christine Shuttleworth, London
Copyedited by Jonathan Fox, Barcelona

Editorial direction: Claudia Stäuble
Project management: Gabriele Ebbecke
Picture editor: Regina Herr
Cover and design: LIQUID, Agentur für Gestaltung, Augsburg
Layout: Andrea Mogwitz, Munich
Production: Astrid Wedemeyer
Art direction: Cilly Klotz
Origination: Reproline Mediateam, Munich
Printing and binding: Druckerei Uhl, Radolfzell

Verlagsgruppe Random House FSC-DEU-0100
The FSC-certified paper *Hello Fat Matt 1,1* has been
supplied by Condat, Le Lardin Saint-Lazare, France.

Printed in Germany

ISBN 978-3-7913-4476-8

*"You have only a short period of
time in your life to make your mark,
and I'm there now."* George Clooney

What is the difference between a well-dressed man and a stunningly dressed woman?
At first glance, very little. Fashionistos like fashionistas choose clothing that accentuates
their best parts, not only of their bodies but also their personalities. Both know when
to follow the rules of style and when to break them. And both have the courage to stay
who they are. But all the same, there is a huge difference. Men have a much easier time
in fashion—and yet a much more difficult one.

Easier, because classic men's fashion has very clear-cut rules; if you follow them, you
can't go wrong. The man who doesn't look good in a custom-made suit of fine fabric has
yet to be born. And if a man also knows the cut that suits him and what accessories are
suitable for what occasion, he has passed an important fashion test. But to make a mark
on the history of style, more is needed—and this is where it gets tricky. Men's fashion does
not suffer rebels gladly. If you have the courage to rebel, you need self-confidence—and
more than that, a sense of style.

Men who dare to break out of the mold have a common denominator: the courage to
show who they are. This, by definition, is where the similarities end. Just as every
fashionisto is an individual, so is his wardrobe. Elegance can blend with defiance, just as
effeminate chic can blend with a rock-star attitude. Everything is permitted, as long as
the mix is characteristic of its wearer—and, ideally, of the zeitgeist. If that is the case, the
result is an intangible flair that elevates a respectably dressed man to a man with true
style.

Simone Werle

THE
GENTLE

EDWARD, DUKE OF WINDSOR
FRED ASTAIRE
FRANK SINATRA
JOHN F. KENNEDY
RALPH LAUREN
JAMES BOND
GEORGE CLOONEY

MEN

EDWARD, DUKE OF WINDSOR

What happens when a king meets the love of his life and she turns out to be wholly unsuitable as a royal consort? In the case of King Edward VIII, monarch of the United Kingdom at the time, the king commits to the woman at his side (in this case the twice-divorced American Wallis Warfield Simpson, who became Duchess of Windsor as a result of their marriage), abdicates for her sake (otherwise Elizabeth II might not be queen today), and spends the rest of his life abroad as a duke, with no official duties. But one thing didn't change a bit: Edward's wardrobe.

"Of course, I do have a slight advantage over the rest of you. It helps in a pinch to be able to remind your bride that you gave up a throne for her."

Even before meeting Wallis Simpson, Edward had the courage of his convictions. Instead of clinging to the rigid style rules of the Victorian age, the monarch preferred innovative clothing combinations, which not only rejuvenated the arch-conservative British gentleman's fashions, but also was the reason for his early reputation as a style icon. Instead of stiff evening dress, Edward favored the tuxedo, which he usually had made in midnight blue. Brown suede shoes complemented his double-breasted suits, most often in a gray chalk stripe that first became really popular when worn by the Duke of Windsor. In fact, everything worn by Edward, who was born in 1894, was immediately copied, and also often named after him. Fair Isle sweaters saw unprecedented demand, plus-fours (today typically worn by golfers) became all the rage, and check-patterned garments became a must even to wear downtown.

Edward, who after his marriage lived primarily in the south of France, was, at the height of his popularity, the most photographed man in the world. And, incidentally, living proof that one need not be king to be the king of his own style.

Edward, Duke
of Windsor, in
a checkered
sports coat with
pleated slacks,
Sunningdale, 1946

In the garden
of the villa in
Biarritz, France.
The Duke wears
a check tie with
his beige suit, 1951

>>
The couple on the
veranda of their
house in Lisbon,
1940. He wears a
gray suit and two-
tone black and
white shoes

Edward, Duke
of Windsor, in
a tuxedo with
a classic white
pocket square
and a carnation
in his lapel, 1960

"He had style. His clothes were always very casual, and terribly, extremely elegant, because he had such taste." Audrey Hepburn

FRED ASTAIRE

He floated across the dance floor as if gravity had no affect on him. A top hat and tails was the signature style of this exceptional dancer, who seemed to have requisitioned elegance for his own exclusive use. Ironically, Fred Astaire put absolutely no stock in his stage appearance. This American legend was in fact the master of the exquisitely casual.

Away from his shows and films, and later also during them, Astaire, born in 1899 as Frederick Austerlitz, the son of an Austrian father and an American mother of German descent, preferred casual clothing. By no means did this mean the entertainer abandoned sophistication or a snappy wardrobe. Astaire preferred day suits, slacks, and sports coats, all custom made on Savile Row (mainly at Anderson and Shepherd). The minimal shoulder padding on his tapered clothing, as well as the small, high-set armholes of his jackets, gave him maximum freedom of movement. In general, Astaire permitted his clothes to neither constrain nor intimidate him. It is said that when he picked up his suits from the tailor, he would hurl them against a wall—to show the clothing (and presumably also his tailor) just who was the boss. And Astaire was just as confident reinterpreting styles according to his own taste.

"The higher up you go, the more mistakes you are allowed. Right at the top, if you make enough of them, it's considered to be your style." Fred Astaire

He frequently mixed strictly traditional British tailoring with unexpected details. Brightly colored socks, impeccably tied cravats (gaily colored and patterned), and fedora hats formed the core of a typical Astaire ensemble. And one can't fail to mention the legendary trademark of the dancer: colorful, patterned neckties worn as belts.

Until his death in 1987, Fred Astaire remained faithful to show business—and to his style.

Elegant in dancing clothes—Fred Astaire in tails with top hat and cane, ca. 1935

In a casual sports coat with boutonnière in a scene from the musical *The Gay Divorcee*, London, 1933

>>
Fred Astaire in a slim-cut suit with bow tie and straw hat for the musical *The Belle of New York*, Los Angeles, 1952

In casual clothes backstage, 1941

FRANK SINATRA

"Trim. Buff. Clean."

For Frank Sinatra, the question of style was crystal clear: "You've either got or you haven't got style. If you got it, you stand out a mile." Sinatra should know—after all, he was way out in front with his look.

*"Don't hide your scars.
They make you who you are."*

Ol' Blue Eyes (Sinatra's eyes were a striking bright blue) was born in 1915 in New Jersey, the son of Italian immigrants. His father, a firefighter, occasional boxer, and bar owner, thought little of his son's plans to become a singer. But when Sinatra Jr. was expelled from school before completing his studies (on the grounds of "general rowdyism"), few options remained open for a truly great future: the choice was between sport, crime, and music. Sinatra decided in favor of the most elegant of the three.

"For me, a tuxedo is a way of life."

In 1935, he won his first talent contest. In the mid-fifties, "The Voice," as he was soon admiringly called, became a star. Sinatra, then as now the prototypical entertainer, attached great importance to his perfect appearance. The list of his clothing rules was as long as his repertoire of number-one hits. In order to ensure the wrinkle-free fit of his custom-made suits, Sinatra avoided sitting down; if this couldn't be avoided, he wouldn't cross his legs. The only acceptable evening color was black. According to Sinatra there was no excuse for wearing gray, blue, or most of all brown after sunset.

*"There's no excuse for brown shoes past sundown ... Or white shoes. Or anything gray, unless it's deep charcoal.
Or blue, unless it's midnight blue. In fact, let's keep it simple: after dark, men should wear black."*

Day or night, his shirt cuffs had to extend exactly one half inch from his jacket sleeves, and his pant legs were only a hair's breadth above his invariably polished shoes. He completed the look with classic monochrome neckties, always silk, precisely folded breast-pocket handkerchiefs, gold cufflinks (but no other jewelry), and a fedora hat. But the singer's most important accessory was the natural ease with which he wore his outfits and which ultimately made his look authentic. It was not for nothing that Sinatra sang: "Style and charm seem to go arm in arm." He was right.

Frank Sinatra in a
black suit, tie, and
Borsalino hat, in a
studio photograph
ca. 1955

JOHN F. KENNEDY

John Fitzgerald Kennedy was the kind of man who appears only once every couple of decades—determined, charismatic, and unmistakably cool. A dazzling aura made the 35th U.S. president into the great shining hope of an entire nation, his appearance a symbol of a new start in a more humane future. And his clothing? He was the best-dressed statesman the world had ever seen.

"Kennedy sets the style, taste, and temper of Washington." GQ, 1961

Yet early on, no one would have predicated John F. Kennedy's transformation into a style icon. His fellow students at college complained of his untidiness, particularly in his attire. At Harvard he was remembered for his ill-fitting suits, tennis shoes, and shirts that never matched his necktie. The turning point came when Jacqueline Bouvier became his wife. She transformed the style of her one true love into that which will remain forever in popular memory.

Kennedy's later outfits were characterized by a clear aesthetic: for public appearances elegantly modern, in private contexts unpretentiously informal, coordinated with casual accessories. Kennedy preferred suits with two-button jackets, a style quite uncommon at the time, in muted colors, often pinstriped, from Brooks Brothers or Savile Row. Born in 1917, the youngest elected president of the United States disliked button-down shirts and loathed wearing hats. Even at his inauguration he declined to don the then customary headwear. Privately, the Democratic statesman wore chinos, blue sport coats, Shetland sweaters, monochrome polo shirts, and penny loafers without socks. Wayfarer sunglasses and convertibles gave him an extra touch of cool.

On November 22, 1963, John F. Kennedy was shot and killed while being driven through Dallas, Texas in an open vehicle. The who and the why of his assassin are still in doubt. Brooks Brothers sells to this day the "Fitzgerald Suit".

John F. Kennedy
as a statesman in
a classic single-
breasted suit

Kennedy on the
yacht *Manitou*
wearing a bright
blue polo shirt and
white linen pants,
Narragansett Bay,
Rhode Island, 1962

>>
In a casual outfit
of Bermudas
and a shirt on
the beach near
the family's
summer home
in Hyannis Port,
Massachusetts,
1953

The three Kennedy
brothers (John,
Robert, and Ted)
in Hyannis Port.
JFK is wearing a
wool sports coat,
white slacks, and
a blue patterned
tie

"It's not about age. It's about taste, and it's about lifestyle." Ralph Lauren

RALPH LAUREN

It is said that he knows more about English style than the English themselves. This certainly has nothing to do with where he comes from. Ralph Lauren was born Ralph Rueben Lifshitz shortly after World War I in the Bronx, one of the more unglamorous boroughs of New York City, as the son of Belorussian Jewish immigrants.

"People ask how can a Jewish kid from the Bronx do preppy clothes? Does it have to do with class and money? It has to do with dreams."

But the boy with the blue eyes knew from an early age where he really belonged: at the top. In a life where the sky always shines ultramarine blue, the sand is pearly white, the lawn is an almost unnatural green, and where the cool languor of the East Coast elite exists amongst

such luxury it seems almost natural. All Lauren needed to reach his goal was the good taste that has remained unchanged to this day.

The Ralph Lauren look is a mixture of dandyish Ivy League chic with early-American legend and an aristocratic English style. Lauren is the grand master of trend-resistant American casual coupled with a hefty dose of European elegance. The self-made American billionaire does not restrict himself to his own wardrobe. He applies his personal style to fashion for women, men, and children, and designs everything necessary—from cosmetics to bed linens—for a "Laurenized" life.

Lauren owns property in Colorado and Jamaica, and an apartment on New York's Fifth Avenue. His vintage car collection is exhibited in museums. The former child of immigrants has realized his dream to an unimaginable extent—not merely with his self-built empire, but above all by living in a world of his own creation. A world so perfect, so embellished, it could never exist in reality—and which, paradoxically, comes across as all the more authentic for that very reason.

Ralph Lauren at his show for Olympus Fashion Week in New York in the fall of 2004. He combines a classic black sports coat with fringed black leather trousers and cowboy boots

Ralph Lauren wears a vest, fringed leather pants, and heavy boots with a loosely knotted silk scarf. Mercedes-Benz Fashion Week, New York, spring 2009

"My name is Bond—James Bond." Sean Connery

JAMES BOND

James Bond, Ian Fleming's fictional British secret agent, has just one mission—to save the world. His work clothes consist of a tuxedo, a suit, skiwear, and perhaps a swimsuit. His accessories are a martini (as a matter of form, shaken not stirred), a pistol (a Walther), and a dangerously beautiful woman guaranteed not to get too attached. All in all, the result is not only a license to kill, but, above all, the perfect model of identification for male fantasy.

In the sixties, Sean Connery portrayed Bond on screen for the first time. The Scottish actor brought to the role a well-toned physique and a male animal sex appeal balanced out by the classic gentleman's wardrobe provided by the English tailor Anthony Sinclair. The central item in 007's wardrobe was a traditional, custom-made suit in Conduit Street style (Conduit Street lies not far from London's more well known Savile Row), usually in gray or blue wool, often woven in Glen plaid. The sport coats, with double back vents, always single-breasted and with two buttons, were noted for their unpretentious cut with a slender torso.

With the introduction of the former car salesman and male model George Lazenby (*On Her Majesty's Secret Service*), the agent's clothing changed.

Under the influence of late-sixties Swinging London, 007 became not only more daring in terms of fashion, but also, given the times, more feminine (in one scene Bond even wears a frilly see-through shirt). Audiences, expecting a hyper-masculine superhero, were bemused. It was a flop, and Lazenby was replaced after just one film. And with him, once again, the wardrobe.

When Roger Moore took on the role he insisted on bringing his personal tailor to the production. With him came casual leisurewear, and thereafter Bond wore more than just his second skin (the custom-made suit). In the Bond role from the sixties to the mid-eighties, he wore safari jackets, casual shirts, and even a banana-yellow ski suit. Apart from this, the color palette was restricted to navy blue, caviar gray, cream, and khaki in all shades. Moore's best outfit? Black slacks and a skintight, black turtleneck sweater, complemented only by a Rolex Submariner watch. Timothy Dalton replaced Moore in the mid-eighties. This somewhat stiff Irishman never really came to terms with his role and was only allowed to play Bond twice. At least he managed to avoid the worst eighties faux pas (an 007 in pastel colors would have been unforgivable). A return to form followed in the nineties with Pierce Brosnan. From then on, Bond has fought his battles

Timothy Dalton in a classic James Bond pose, 1987

Sean Connery in a custom-made suit as a laid-back Bond leaning on a car, ca. 1970

Roger Moore and Jane Seymour in *Live and Let Die*. James Bond wears a tan sports coat with black slacks, 1973 neither in traditional English-tailored clothing nor in the latest fashions, but in classic Brioni custom-made suits costing five thousand dollars each, as if self-confident masculinity had been transformed into cloth, influenced only by the time's "minimal chic." Further innovations were a dark leather jacket and an Omega Seamaster Quartz watch.

The Bond of the new millennium, in the person of Daniel Craig, is not only the first blond Bond, but also the most contradictory. In line with the developments in society and pop culture, Bond fights harder, is more physical, but also harbors more self-doubt. His outfits are typically casual (always emphasizing the biceps); the suits are debonair, with a notable accent on his masculine physique. It will be fascinating to see what comes next.

George Lazenby as an effeminate Bond in a ruffled shirt, with Diana Rigg in *On Her Majesty's Secret Service*, 1969

Pierce Brosnan in a heroic pose wearing a classic three-piece suit with no tie, 1997

Daniel Craig with a Colt pistol, tuxedo, and bow tie for the Bond film Casino Royale, 2005

GEORGE
CLOONEY

It is said that stars will forever behave like the age at which they achieve fame. Luckily, George Clooney was more than forty years old when he shot to stardom in the mid-nineties as a smart television doctor. Today, no one wears suits with as much natural elegance and charmingly masculine self-assurance as this actor, who at times seems to be of an earlier era.

"You have only a short period of time in your life to make your mark, and I'm there now."

According to Clooney, his best feature is his chin. "I just have a good old chin," the actor once said in an interview. But perfect features alone are not enough to complement a sophisticated gentleman's outfit. One thing is needed above all—charisma, a trait Clooney has worked hard to cultivate. In reality, this actor and filmmaker, named several times the "Sexiest Man Alive," employs a sharp mind to give substance to his roles. It is the blend of sex appeal and intellect that makes this show-biz veteran and gentleman a style icon.

Clooney's style is an update of old Hollywood with a dose of European modernism, a classic down to every detail. The typical Clooney look is constructed around precisely tailored dark suits and plain white dress shirts, or medium-gray slacks combined with simple, light-colored shirts. The frequent absence of a necktie proves that good style does not mean one must give up personal choice or comfort.

His best outfit: the tuxedo. Though Clooney has been treading the red carpet for years wearing the same Armani evening suit, no other item of clothing so clearly represents the essence of Clooney—nothing more is needed.

George Clooney in his
tux at the 63rd Golden
Globes, Los Angeles,
2006

At the Venice Film
Festival in a discreetly
striped open shirt under
a dark-blue sports coat,
2009

THE
REBEL

MARLON BRANDO
CHE GUEVARA
STEVE MCQUEEN
JAMES DEAN
JOHNNY CASH
KURT COBAIN

s

"There's a line in the picture where he snarls, 'Nobody tells me what to do.' That's exactly how I've felt all my life."

MARLON BRANDO

Marlon Brando did not try to provoke—he was provocation personified. The actor did not emote for his roles, but rather threw his entire being into them. Brando's facial expressions and style spoke louder than did most of his colleagues with pages of dialogue.

"I know I'm not an easy person to get along with. I'm no walk in the park."

Brando was born in 1924 in rural America, to a mother fascinated by amateur theater and a largely absentee father. Rather than sharing a love for their child, his parents shared a love of alcohol. Brando was seventeen when he was thrown out of military school and nineteen when he fled to New York City to become an actor. And although he spurned advice to get his striking nose fixed, in no time at all Brando became the idol and sex symbol of an entire nation.

The handsome actor's face expressed the pent-up emotions then welling within an entire postwar generation; his clothing represented an urgently desired new beginning. The more simply Brando dressed, the better he looked. A light-gray, sweat-soaked t-shirt with slightly rolled-up sleeves, stretched taut over his muscular body, jeans, and a leather jacket: nothing else was needed to transform the Hollywood actor into a tough rebel with the devastating eroticism of an anti-hero. When he was asked in the movie *The Wild One* exactly what he was rebelling against, Brando replied, "What have you got?"

"America has been good to me, but that wasn't a gift."

It would be another two decades before Brando was finally tamed. He was restyled, dressed up, even dandified. The price was a career and a life like a roller-coaster ride, reaching the highest heights and the lowest depths. Brando, who married several times, died in 2004 at the age of eighty.

Marlon Brando combines a simple cotton t-shirt with a bracelet and a cigarette, ca. 1955

>>
In peaked cap, t-shirt, and dark leather jacket in *The Wild One*, 1953

Brando reading the script for the movie The Men in his bathrobe, Los Angeles, 1949

CHE GUEVARA

Slightly windswept hair beneath a starred felt beret and a plain, military-style shirt to match; a handsome face with flawless features outlined by a sparse beard; the gaze, resolute yet dreamy, fixed toward the future. When one thinks today of revolution, the image of Che Guevara automatically comes to mind. And that image in particular.

"Many will call me an adventurer—and that I am, only one of a different sort: one of those who risks his skin to prove his platitudes."

Alberto Korda, the creator of probably the most frequently reproduced photograph of all time, recalls the moment he took it: "I remember it as if it were today ... seeing him framed in the viewfinder, with that expression. I am still startled by the impact ... it shakes me so powerfully." Korda instinctively took a step backward and pressed the shutter twice in quick succession. It was 1960, and the image was recorded for posterity. A palm tree and a truncated profile at the edge of the photograph were retouched. Nothing was

to detract from the magnetic charisma of the thirty-one-year-old Guevara, who at the time was serving as president of the national bank after the successful Cuban revolution. But the picture was to lie hidden in the photographer's desk drawer for another seven years.

In 1967, the Argentine Ernesto "Che" Guevara set off to repeat his revolutionary activities in Bolivia. In Cuba, shortly before, as Fidel Castro's minister of industries he helped push the country's economy into a swift decline. Guevara failed in Bolivia and was summarily executed. And it was for this that he became immortal. Since then his image has adorned everything from posters to cigarette lighters. For posterity, the Communist guerrilla fighter forever remains a stunningly good-looking, very young man with big ideals—regardless of the fact that he ordered thousands of executions, some of which he personally carried out. His potential for inspiring fear has long been superseded by a romantically transfigured image. What remains is Che, a pop star of youthful revolution, completely divorced from reality.

Che Guevara as *Guerrillero Heroico*, 1960

44

*"The Steve McQueen I knew was
a man of simple tastes. He wore jeans,
lumberjack shirts, chukka boots,
and trucker hats."*
Barbara McQueen

STEVE MCQUEEN

There are men who can wear anything and invariably still look good. One such person was Steve McQueen. The American actor not only actually wore almost everything, from a racing jacket to a sailor suit, but he always looked exactly as every man wishes they could—supremely cool and uncompromisingly masculine. Steve McQueen, the most laid-back guy in American film history, never once considered apologizing for what he was. And that was how he looked.

The style legacy McQueen left is simple. Classic items such as aviator sunglasses, black turtleneck sweaters, slim-cut suits, khaki pants, windbreakers, and shawl-collar cardigans were as much part of the amateur race-car driver McQueen's repertoire as simple cotton t-shirts, check shirts, leather jackets, jeans, and heavy boots. But it was not primarily the clothing that transformed the actor into a style icon. It was the way he wore them.

McQueen combined classic American sportswear with the gritty, sometimes melancholic authenticity of the gutsy outsider.

Whether with fashion or films, McQueen cared little for the opinions of others—perhaps because he had already seen more than most of his Hollywood colleagues. He was born in 1930 in Indianapolis to an alcoholic mother and a stunt pilot father he never knew. He described his childhood laconically as "the earliest shit," and until his big break on Broadway he got by with odd jobs and a stretch in the Marines. It was undoubtedly those tough early years that molded his resolute demeanor, which demanded neither too many words nor too many details. And it was probably those youthful shadows that cast the most light on Steve McQueen's instinctive style.

Steve McQueen in a sweater and light, worn jeans as Virgil Hilts in *The Great Escape*, 1963

Casual outfit with half-open denim shirt, ca. 1970

Black turtleneck sweater with a holster in *Bullitt*, 1968

JAMES DEAN

James Dean is not simply a movie legend. James Dean is the prototypical King of Cool. To reach this status, the young American needed surprisingly little: twenty-four years of life, four completed films—and a simple white t-shirt.

"Dream as if you'll live forever.
Live as if you'll die today."

In fact, by the mid-fifties this white article of clothing had long been a staple in society—as an undershirt. The Marines had officially adopted the t-shirt as standard issue attire during World War II, and exactingly defined the cut and construction: round neckline, sleeves set at right angles to the body, and pure white cotton. Though Marlon Brando was the first to wear the undershirt as an outer garment, it was James Dean who fully exploited the white tee's potential. What he wore it with was not important—typically straight-leg dark blue jeans, a simple red windbreaker, and mildly tousled hair combed up-wards—it was his attitude that moved the youth of the buttoned-up fifties toward collective rebellion. Dean, born in 1931 in a small town in Indiana, needed neither words nor expensive threads to rouse the longings of his generation, to handsomely embody the eternal struggle between the young and the old. His gaze (a mixture of shy vulnerability and youthful pride), his stance (casual, mostly with his hands in his jeans pockets and the ubiquitous cigarette in the corner of his mouth), and that white t-shirt, were enough to convey the message: I'm not like you, I don't want to be like you, I don't even dig your clothes. Ever since James Dean, just about every teenage idol wanting to be taken seriously has based his look on the James Dean model.

"The only greatness for man
is immortality."

On September 30, 1955, the actor's gleaming silver Porsche 550 Spyder collided with student Donald Turnupseed's blue Ford. James Dean died instantly. His legacy is immortal.

James Dean with tousled hair in a t-shirt, jeans, and a red windbreaker, 1955

>>
Dean with his shirt casually unbuttoned during the filming of *Giant*, 1955

Posing in a white cotton t-shirt and jeans for the movie *Rebel Without a Cause*, Los Angeles, 1955

JOHNNY CASH

Every time he appeared, he greeted his audience in the same way: "Hello, I'm Johnny Cash." What he meant was: I'm here and you're not alone any more. I don't belong anywhere, but this evening I belong just to you. The American was the antithesis of the clean-cut country singer. Johnny Cash was authentic. And so were his clothes.

"I love to wear a rainbow every day / And tell the world that everything's o.k. / But I'll try to carry off a little darkness on my back. / Till things are brighter, I'm the Man in Black."

Beginning in the early seventies, Cash wore just one color on stage: black. It was liberating. It meant that the "Man in Black" could stand visually apart from the colorful, kitschy country and western style of most of his colleagues. Cash chose the darkest of all tones (he favored leather coats or well-worn shirts) to show with whom he identified—society's outsiders. "I wear the black for the poor and the beaten down / Livin' in the hopeless, hungry side of town," was how Cash explained his choice of color in one of his songs,

"I wear it for the prisoner who has long paid for his crime / But is there because he's a victim of the times."

"Sometimes I am two people. Johnny is the nice one. Cash causes all the trouble. They fight."

Though Cash himself was never incarcerated for long, he nevertheless knew of what he spoke. Born the son of Arkansas farmers in 1932, his father gave him a tough upbringing (including heavy physical labor). Later, the sensitive spirit of this exceptionally talented artist would react to his meteoric rise to fame with a drug and alcohol addiction that nearly cost him his career and his life. It was only through June Carter that he found the way back—first to his talent and finally to himself. His brilliant comeback concert at Folsom Prison remains unforgettable. It was not the old Johnny Cash singing to the inmates on the prison stage, but the newborn "Man in Black." And he put his heart into it.

Johnny Cash
dressed in black,
ca. 1957

On stage at the Grand Gala du Disque,
Amsterdam, 1972

"I'd rather be hated for who I am, than loved for who I am not."

KURT COBAIN

"Rather be dead than cool."

He was the reluctant anti-hero of Generation X, and in the end fell victim to his success. In the early nineties Kurt Cobain set off a musical landslide with the birth of grunge, a new musical style merging the sound of seventies rock with the punk spirit. Millions of teenagers, unsettled by the social developments of the time, wanted to be just like the lead singer in Nirvana: sensitive but angry, fragile yet brave enough to be different. The check flannel shirt symbolized the movement.

"We're so trendy we can't even escape ourselves."

Cobain's style of dress suited his music: tattered, unaffected, and always consistent. His favorite article of clothing was a green check shirt, of which he had several. In the state of Washington, where Cobain was born in 1967 (it was out of Seattle that grunge became popular), this simple garment had for years been popular as work clothes. Cobain's shirts were always faded and often at least one size too big. It seemed

he picked up his look at the Salvation Army. Cobain's outfits also featured faded, open cardigans, oversized t-shirts, torn and faded Levi's, and worn-out Chuck Taylors. The chin-length blond hair and ever-present three-day beard framed the face of the heroin-addled Cobain. Together with the deeply melancholic blue eyes, this was a mix that couldn't fail to influence the youth of the early nineties.

Kurt Cobain was twenty-seven years old when he took his own life with a shotgun on April 5, 1994. In his suicide note he quoted Neil Young: "It's better to burn out than to fade away." After his death, the anti-hero who never found his place in the world became a legend. In the list of the "top-earning dead artists," he took over first place, supplanting even Elvis.

"The worst crime is faking it."

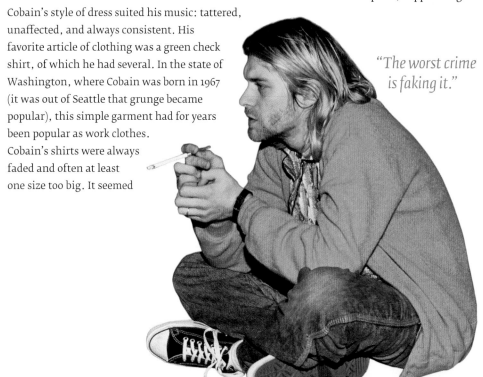

"Wanting to be someone else is a waste of the person you are."

Kurt Cobain relaxing with a cigarette in a mustard-yellow cardigan, jeans, and Chuck Taylors, 1990

On stage with Nirvana for *MTV Live and Loud* in a military-style jacket, 1993

At *MTV Unplugged* in a worn, moss-colored cardigan, New York, 1993

THE DAND

OSCAR WILDE
GIANNI AGNELLI
TRUMAN CAPOTE
TOM WOLFE
BRYAN FERRY
ANDRÉ LEON TALLEY
FALCO
ANDRÉ BENJAMIN
LAPO ELKANN

IES

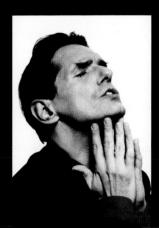

OSCAR WILDE

"You see, Phipps, fashion is what one wears oneself.
What is unfashionable is what other people wear."

He was an acclaimed writer, an admired dandy, a pop star among intellectuals, and in the end bourgeois society had its revenge for his flamboyant lifestyle. Hardly anyone has fallen as deep and as suddenly as Oscar Wilde, for hardly anyone could have reached such heights in the first place. His intellectual superiority, his unfaltering courage to be extravagant, and his artistic legacy are, in retrospect, as splendid as his precipitous downfall into the filth of the Victorian Reading Jail was tragic.

"I have the simplest tastes. I am always
satisfied with the best."

Wilde was born in 1854 in Dublin—to the disappointment of his mother, for Lady Wilde had longed for a girl. It was said that despite little Oscar's male gender she often clothed him in dresses and delicate blouses. Later, during his studies at Oxford, Wilde attracted attention, first for his clothes (his preferred fabrics even in his early years were velvet, furs, and silk), and then for his verbal wit. At twenty-three this bird of paradise conquered the London salons. Wilde was not a handsome man, but one of remarkable elegance who knew how to present himself. He did not follow fashion, but

rather defined it. He would walk through Piccadilly Circus holding a white lily, his brown hair waving, and covered in a purple cloak; or would hold forth on aesthetics while wearing velvet knee-breeches, a lavender striped silk jacket, and lace cuffs.

"Fashion is a form of ugliness so intolerable
that we have to alter it every six months."

In 1895, Wilde, who had become a celebrated dramatist, was sentenced to prison with hard labor for homosexual offences. After his arrest, he was finished in every respect. His property was sold at auction, his paternal rights over his two sons withdrawn, and his work (including *The Picture of Dorian Gray, Salome,* and *The Importance of Being Earnest*) obliterated from public memory. Oscar Wilde died at the age of forty-six in Paris. When one of his few remaining friends offered him a last glass of champagne, he is said to have commented, "I am dying as I have lived: beyond my means."

Oscar Wilde in a white suit with hat and cane, 1884

In velvet jacket and knee-breeches, 1882

>>
Wilde with wide-brimmed hat and dark cape, 1882

In "thinker" pose with a fur-trimmed coat and a walking stick, 1882

GIANNI AGNELLI

Comparing Giovanni (known as Gianni) Agnelli with the twentieth century's other great industrialists, one notices certain similarities: dizzying wealth, tremendous business acumen, and enormous political influence. What distinguished this tycoon from Turin from his powerful colleagues? Agnelli had style.

Signor Agnelli, "L'Avvocato," master playboy and head of the Italian Fiat empire (his grandfather, Giovanni Agnelli, Sr., founded the Fabbrica Italiana Automobili Torino in 1899), quickly attracted attention with his look. Anyone who thought anything of themselves in the Italian jet set wanted to look like "Dottore Fiat." The foundation of a typical Agnelli outfit was relatively easy to imitate: a custom-made suit (preferably by Caraceni) in a classic cut and constructed of the finest cloth. When it came to styling, Agnelli proved that he had the courage to indulge his individuality.

Flashy watches worn over shirt cuffs, tall suede boots with dark-blue flannel pinstripe suits, and cashmere neckties dangling under the jacket but over the sweater: Gianni Agnelli truly never shrank from any supposed stylistic faux pas. For as the tall magnate knew from his business life: only those who have the courage to break the rules are rewarded with success. Despite his quirks, Agnelli's look was always serious and inherently consistent—but without sacrificing any of his individuality. A few more legendary classics of the Agnelli fashion repertoire: unbuttoned buttons (on shirt cuffs, collars, and at the bottom of his shirt), neckties clearly worn too short (often silk knit or patterned), and button-down collar shirts (preferably from Brooks Brothers) with a double-breasted jacket.

In 2003, Giovanni Agnelli died at the age of eighty-one after a long illness. He bequeathed all his custom-made suits to his grandson Lapo Elkann.

Gianni Agnelli in
a classic summer
suit, 1968

With a dotted silk
tie and a watch
worn over the
cuff, 1968

TRUMAN CAPOTE

"There has never been anyone like me and there will never be anyone like me again."

In the 1950s, someone like Truman Capote could only have survived in New York City. He was a sharp-witted party king, acclaimed dandy of literature, and brilliant monster, all at once. Anywhere else he would probably have been a simple outsider, and the only attention given to him would have been surreptitious whispers. But in Manhattan he could be anything at all. At least until high society slammed the door in his face.

"I don't care what anybody says about me as long as it isn't true."

That Capote was different from most of his fellow human beings was apparent even in childhood—to the great displeasure of his mother, LilliMae, who was a mere teenager with a salacious history when he was born in 1924. Named Truman Streckfus Persons, he was almost girlishly soft, with gentle, undefined features and fine white-blond hair. His behavior suited his appearance. Even as a child, Capote was avid for attention and over-sensitive, with a tendency to write down his each and every thought. No, he didn't quite fit in New Orleans. At age fifteen the boy ended up in New York. The city was to be his stage.

The newcomer lost no time rising in society. His weapons were literary success, a sharp tongue, and a healthy dose of style. When the "Tiny Terror" (Capote was only 5′ 3″ tall) appeared in public, he dressed exclusively in the finest threads and without fear of accessories (his favorites being a lightweight silk scarf and a white hat with a contrasting dark band). Capote was indisputably an artist, and his own person was his work of art, which in the end he himself destroyed.

"Well, I'm about as tall as a shotgun, and just as noisy."

New York society, which in 1966 had scrambled for invitations to his Black and White Ball, promptly shunned him when his society novel *Answered Prayers* turned out to be a tell-all roman à clef. Capote made the mistake of sawing off the branch onto which he had so nimbly and with great effort climbed. The once pampered fair-haired boy spent his final years in isolation and permanent intoxication. He died of an overdose in 1984.

Truman Capote
combines a dark
jacket with a light
vest and slacks,
1947

>>
Capote
accessorizes
his airy summer
look with black
loafers, a bracelet,
and a cigarette,
ca. 1950

In tails with a top
hat and a rose
boutonnière, 1973

TOM WOLFE

Can a man who wears the same thing every day become a style icon? He can, but only if his name is Tom Wolfe, and only if that "same thing" is a custom-tailored white suit.

"Men over 35 who go around without neckties must be crazy."

What is most remarkable is that his memorable look is actually the fruit of a mistake. Wolfe, born in 1931 in the southern United States, settled in New York in the early sixties to work as a journalist. Shortly before relocating, the Yale graduate ordered a custom-made suit in honor of his big move—in brilliant white. Though a white suit is customarily worn in the summer in his home state of Virginia, it was rather inappropriate for the streets of New York City. Worse still, Wolfe, still inexperienced in matters of clothing, had chosen for the suit a fabric too heavy for summer,

and out of necessity wore his dazzling outfit during the metropolis's dirty, gray winter. But he didn't get lost in the snow. On the contrary, friends and colleagues, even passing strangers, reacted with scorn and let forth with streams of abuse at the young intellectual—a reaction that fit Wolfe to a tee. Even at that time, the founder of "New Journalism" and later bestselling author (his first novel *The Bonfire of the Vanities* was a global success) relished the role of a socially conservative maverick. His suit became a uniform. Today, more than forty versions of it hang in the adopted New Yorker's closet, often three-piece, mostly double-breasted, and always custom-made. He only varies his accessories. Wolfe prefers patterned shirts, color neckties (he is never seen without a tie), breast-pocket handkerchiefs, and two-tone shoes. Wolfe himself feels that his suit simply saves time and trouble: "I just stand there, people talk to me, I say almost nothing, and in the end they rush off to tell their friends, 'That Tom Wolfe really is an incredibly interesting man.'"

Tom Wolfe in a
white three-piece
suit with bow
tie, breast-pocket
handkerchief, and
two-tone shoes,
2005

Wolfe in front
of his house,
New York, 1968

*"Why should I spoil my mood
by wearing an ugly suit?"*

BRYAN FERRY

"Sometimes it's a real pain," confessed Bryan Ferry, "People would rather ask me about my socks than about my music." While true that there are few musicians asked as often about his style of clothing as the front man of Roxy Music, one can hardly blame the journalists. For in the world of music, Bryan Ferry is quite simply the personification of the custom-made suit.

*"You stop looking at beautiful women
when you're dead. Presumably."*

His fashion sense certainly has nothing to do with his background. He was born in 1945 in Washington, a drab, working-class town in the northeast of England. Young Bryan loved his parents, but he knew that the life of his coalminer father would not be his own—in fact, he had already adopted the look of the jazz musicians he so admired. Ferry wanted to wear a suit and shirt rather than the standard leather jacket and jeans of the time. At age fifteen he began to work as a casual assistant to a tailor, using his pay to buy records, shoes, and narrow neckties.

Then, in the early seventies, came the founding of the band Roxy Music, which, though missing for a time, has never officially broke up. Their very first recording made the Top Five, and Ferry impressed both fans and critics with a whole new sound—glam rock. Decadence had never before been an element of rock music, much less the look of the well-groomed Englishman, who faced the cameras in tiger-patterned jackets, platform boots, long hair, and clearly wearing makeup. Later—and until this very day—came appearances in perfectly fitting custom-made suits, combined with extravagant accessories, lightly blow-dried hair, a furtive gaze, and at least one beautiful woman at his side.

*"With men's fashion, it's a question of
details. Women have all the fun."*

"Actually we were never really rock stars," Ferry commented at one point in an interview. "While other bands smashed up their hotel rooms, we preferred to worry about how we could make them look more beautiful." He no longer needs to concern himself about his own look.

Bryan Ferry in a gray one-button custom-made suit, photographed at the Sanderson Hotel, 2003

Wearing a white double-breasted suit, denim shirt, and dotted scarf, Manchester, 1973

Roxy Music's frontman in a London recording studio, 1972

ANDRÉ LEON TALLEY

"My coats are like a teepee that could house a family of Lilliputians."

This man is the heavyweight of the fashion world. It is not merely because André Leon Talley, standing 6' 7" tall, of daunting girth, and with a size 13 shoe, has towered over his colleagues for more than thirty years at fashion shows from Paris to Milan. More than anything else it is his enormous influence that has made him a star of the industry. This mighty giant with an even larger ego makes or breaks entire careers with his razor-sharp commentary. Anyone who has been praised by him in his column "Life with André" (previously "André's Stylefax") in American *Vogue* has made it. Anyone who doesn't even get a mention simply needs to try harder.

Talley was born into a modest background in 1949 in a small North Carolina town. In spite of meager resources, as a child he began to learn from his grandmother, who raised him by herself, the value and meaning of luxury—a sense he carries always. Talley, who as a young man began to devour *Vogue* each month, and who had occasionally worked for

Andy Warhol for fifty dollars a week, knows no limits when choosing his wardrobe. His credo is not to be afraid of colors, prints, or fabrics, and certainly not of absolute luxury. The American designer is living proof that the vanity of fashion journalists must by no means lag behind that of designers. Voluminous fur scarves, tent-size metallic jackets, skunk-fur capes, purple alligator boots, and egg-yolk yellow jogging suits in mirrored velvet are as normal in the world of André Leon Talley as his obligatory sunglasses, which, like his mentor Anna Wintour, he very rarely takes off. As different as the pieces in his wardrobe are, they all have one thing in common: highly concentrated eccentricity, and a guarantee they come from a high-end luxury house.

In a world that thrives on what one is on the outside, Talley has for decades followed a secret yet simple recipe: only the craziest of the eccentrics is immune to falling victim to it.

André Leon Talley wearing a shiny kimono in heavy silk and black patent-leather buckle shoes at a gala dinner after the Valentino fashion show, Rome, 2007

Talley in a fur-trimmed collar and mirrored sunglasses, on the phone at Olympus Fashion Week, fall 2006

In a mustard silk cape and a gold chain with an animal-tooth pendant at a breakfast at the 21 Club, New York, 2010

FALCO

He was so uncompromisingly dandified that one could even sense his arrogance in photographs. Falco was the first German-speaking rapper and, before the term even existed, one of the world's first yuppies. His trademark was incredibly stylish threads flaunted with cool petulance.

"He was a superstar, he was popular. He was so eccentric because he had flair. He was a virtuoso, a rock idol. And everyone was shouting: Come on and rock me Amadeus."

Born in 1957 as Johann Hölzl in Vienna's fifth district, while still in kindergarten Falco snapped his fingers so enthusiastically to the music on the radio that his mother immediately signed him up for piano lessons. When he was ready to go to school, the boy had a repertoire of more than thirty songs, and a teacher at a music competition certified him as having perfect pitch. It was a good thing, too, for Hölzl made his career choice at an early age: he wanted to be a pop star. He left school early to pursue his goal, joined a succession of bands as a bass player, and promptly began to create a sensation with his outfits.

Instead of appearing in the fashion of the time with long hair, jeans, and a disheveled look, the Austrian walked onstage in the late seventies with short, slicked-back hair, sunglasses, a silver and black striped suit, and a dark leather coat. His frank explanation: "That's how it is, I'm Falco now." Falco was the essence of the eighties before they began. During appearances he protected his Versace suits and Fiorucci sweaters from his messy bandmates with plastic wrap. The early eighties saw his breakthrough as a solo artist. Songs such as "Der Kommissar," "Rock Me Amadeus," and "Jeannie" catapulted the eccentric tuxedo-clad singer onto the global pop charts. And yet, he wasn't exactly lovable. In fact, he was rather narcissistic and megalomaniacal, just right for a time when "yuppie" was not yet a term of abuse.

In February 1998, Falco died as a consequence of a traffic accident in the Caribbean, where he had secluded himself to work on his comeback from drug and alcohol problems, personal failures, and a profound lack of hit records. His posthumously released album propelled him once again to the top of the charts.

Falco photographed in a black leather cape for the album cover of *Nachtflug,* 1992

ANDRÉ BENJAMIN

Ever since Run-D.M.C., it seems pretty clear how a hip-hop star should look: heavy jewelry, fabulous clothes, plus an even bigger attitude. Hold on—someone stepped out of line. André Benjamin (also known as André 3000) simply refuses to dip into the wardrobe that works so well for other hip-hop artists. The reward for his disregard: enormous success.

"Cool is not just one type of cool. Cool is confidence and knowing, what you are and being fine with it."

Born in Atlanta, André Lauren Benjamin was the only child of a single mother. First learning violin, then several other instruments, the boy's classical music education did not stop him from participating in schoolyard rap battles. His favorite sparring partner in those wars of verbosity became the rapper Antwan "Big Boi," with whom he founded the hip-hop duo Outkast. As Benjamin's self-confidence

grew alongside the success of their albums, he began to adopt his own style. The result has been a continuous evolution away from the stereotypical rapper image, yet without sacrificing any of his credibility.

Benjamin favors vintage English fashion, building upon rich colors, patterns (particularly large-scale plaids), and a mix of classic and surprising accessories. His style is a good-humored, urbane tour of historic styles, themes, and motifs that, combined and camouflaged, make it nearly impossible to identify an outfit's origins. Benjamin can wear busy form-fitting shirts and tartan plaid pants with white leather gloves, suspenders, and elegant two-tone shoes without being the least bit self-conscious.

"Now what's cooler than bein' cool? Ice Cold!"

Much more than an affected show-off, this Southern dandy exudes creative individuality. And in the process, his wardrobe sends a message that even a grade-school violinist can become a hip-hop megastar. Provided you stay true to yourself.

André Benjamin poses for photos in black knickers, geranium-red vest and matching socks, a black newsboy cap, and sunglasses during the MTV Europe Music Awards in 2004 in Rome

André Benjamin in a farmer's hat, neckerchief, and skull-pattern suspenders at a film premiere in New York, 2005

LAPO ELKANN

Does good style run in the family? In the case of Lapo Elkann, definitely. For this darling of the jet set, born in 1977, not only inherited the legendary made-to-measure suits of his grandfather Gianni Agnelli, but seems to have acquired along with them the outsize sense of style and the courageous, perfectly honed eccentricity.

"My luxury is simplicity."

Even chilly fashion divas such as Anna Wintour, editor in chief of American *Vogue,* rave about the Fiat heir's fashion sense. But the "most elegant man on the planet" (according to Wintour) wants nothing to do with his fame as a style icon. "I am not a fashionisto. I don't like to talk about what I wear. I wear what I feel like at the time." Of course, this is precisely the Italian's strength: wearing exactly what he feels like wearing.

Looks put together by Lapo Elkann are almost always an exciting mix of made-to-measure conservative classics (his suits invariably feature trademark wide lapels), bright colors from azure blue to Amalfi lemon yellow, and, just like his grandfather, capricious details (Elkann's favorite shoes are embroidered velvet slippers, worn without socks). The noble dandy with the notoriously unruly, strawberry blond mane is not afraid of crossing the boundaries of so-called good taste, or indeed of redefining just where those boundaries are. While what Lapo Elkann wears may seem too loud north of the Alps, to the south each outfit is received with gleeful anticipation, idealized, and copied. Elkann gives a long-marginalized Italy with a new dose of fashionable self-confidence.

"I'm no fashionisto."

The 2005 drug scandal that nearly cost Elkann his life is ancient history. But he has learned from the incident. "There have been moments in life that forced me to look at myself more than I normally do. I am a straight shooter; I don't like easy compromises. Above all, I don't like mediocrity." One can tell just by looking at him.

Lapo Elkann attends
a dinner wearing an
ultramarine jacket with
white trim and blue velvet
loafers, Milan, 2010

With a scarf and glen plaid
blazer at the premiere of
The Pursuit of Happyness
at the Auditorium
Conciliazione, Rome, 2007

THE
ROCK
STARS

JIMI HENDRIX
MICK JAGGER
FREDDIE MERCURY
JARVIS COCKER

*"I used to live in a room full of mirrors /
All I could see was me. / I take my
spirit and I crash my mirrors / Now
the whole world is here for me to see."*

JIMI HENDRIX

At first glance, his biography seems no different than that of any number of rock stars. First the difficult childhood, during which, in spite of the circumstances, the musician discovered his love for his instrument. Then came the struggle for recognition, followed by the meteoric rise to the heights of music. And finally, the precipitous decline to the untimely end expected and required of true legends. What distinguishes Jimi Hendrix's journey through life from that of so many others? His style: both of his guitar playing and his look.

*"All I'm gonna do is just go
on and do what I feel."*

Hendrix was seventeen years old when he bought his first electric guitar. Born in Seattle in 1942, the American bluesman started out as a sideman for various artists, duly playing the correct notes and toiling in obscurity. But leaving the spotlight to others was not part of Hendrix's character, and he took off to England with the hopes of making it as a solo artist.

One of the few appliances in his meager luggage was a set of hair curlers.

With his playing technique (Hendrix knew no limits—playing on his back and with his tongue—anything went) and his new sound (exploring the sonic possibilities of feedback, overlapping frequencies, and distortion), the young musician soon made his mark on the scene. He spent his first paycheck not on music, but on his look. His early stage outfits consisted of army uniforms and hussars' jackets decorated with armbands and brooches. Later, when Hendrix's success re-crossed the Atlantic to the United States (his performance at Woodstock is legendary), he extended his style to flared pants, embroidered brocade vests, psychedelic patterned shirts, wide-brimmed hats, bandanas (which he supposedly soaked in LSD), and lots of jewelry, especially necklaces with medallions. His style had a decisive influence on the look of the hippies, who worshipped him like an idol.

*"You have to go on and be crazy.
Craziness is like heaven."*

This was exactly what Hendrix couldn't handle. At a mere twenty-seven years of age, the musician succumbed to a fatal combination of sleeping pills and alcohol. The exact circumstances of his death have never been fully explained.

Jimi Hendrix on stage at the Royal Albert Hall in a silk shirt with kimono sleeves and skintight pants, London, 1969

Jimi Hendrix surrounded by ornately embroidered brocade fabric, 1967

MICK JAGGER

One does not necessarily have to look masculine to be a male sex symbol. Mick Jagger is a perfect example. Standing just 5′ 9″, the British singer has slender arms, even thinner legs, and hips the width of a schoolboy. Jagger's physique is not just androgynous; it is almost extraterrestrial. And yet for decades this gaunt man has been the very image of the ultimate rock star.

The beginnings of the Jagger style were anything but promising. The sixties already had in the Beatles its music and fashion gurus. But together with his schoolmate Keith Richards, Jagger, born in 1943 the son of a physics teacher, set out—after abandoning his business studies—to counterbalance the clean-living image of the Fab Four. In 1965, with their hard blues-rock and bad-boy attitudes, the Rolling Stones and their front man Mick Jagger broke through with their first hit "(I Can't Get No) Satisfaction."

"It doesn't matter if you're starting out or you're doing it for years. There's no point in having a huge dress-up if you're playing a 500-seat club. And if you're playing for 50,000 people, there's no point in wearing rags."

Jagger represented something completely new: frenetic, transgressive, and, above all, unashamedly flaunted sexuality. The look accompanying this controversial image unequivocally blurred the boundaries between the sexes. Mick Jagger pranced anthropomorphically across the stage in dangerously dark eyeliner, dangling gold earrings, and scruffy chin-length hair complemented by skintight one-piece Ossie Clark jumpsuits slit to the navel (complete with frills and rhinestones); or graphically patterned t-shirts and pants so tight they seemed to have been sprayed directly onto his body.

Nothing has ever changed in the musician's style. Even more surprisingly, after forty years in show business Mick Jagger's look has lost none of its authenticity or its ability to capture the spirit of his time.

Mick Jagger
on stage in
Rotterdam in a
white Ossie Clark
jumpsuit and a
metallic belt, 1973

Jagger in a tight
black t-shirt at
the Super Bowl XL
Halftime Show,
Detroit, 2006

"The reason we're successful, darling? My overall charisma, of course."

"I won't be a rock star. I will be a legend."

FREDDIE MERCURY

"I dress to kill, but tastefully."

Anyone who has ever saw Freddie Mercury in concert never forgets it. Gazing up toward the sky, legs spread or preparing to pirouette, one combatively clenched fist outstretched, the other hand grasping the half-length microphone stand that swirled away from his hairy chest like a lightning rod: that was the lead singer of Queen. And then, when he belted out "We Are The Champions" or "We Will Rock You" with his four-octave vocal range, the atmosphere among the public would finally boil over into a frenzy.

"I have fun with my clothes onstage; it's not a concert you're seeing, it's a fashion show."

Freddie Mercury was born Farrokh Bulsara in Zanzibar in 1946, but his real home was to be the stage. One of the world's most successful rock 'n' roll stories began in the early seventies in London. Mercury, together with Roger Taylor and Brian May, founded Queen, and were soon to be joined by John Deacon. Mercury came up with the band's name, and designed the logo and stage costumes with a clear style in mind. From the very beginning, Queen moved between rock and opera with a pronounced aesthetic sense of

theatrical drama that would only grow over the following two decades.

In the seventies Mercury wore his hair long and his stage outfits skin-tight. His low-cut leotards were an appealing mix of girlish ballerina charm and tough machismo. Mercury succeeded in blurring the borders without appearing androgynous. In the eighties, his outfits became more athletic, his hair shorter, and his mustache an essential feature of his rock-star look. What remained were the extravagant leather and spandex creations, always skin-tight, always drawing attention to his crotch.

"I always knew I was a star. And now, the rest of the world seems to agree with me."

Alcohol, drugs, countless affairs and flings, and as much partying as one could fit in a day finally took their toll. In 1991, Freddie Mercury died at the age of forty-five in London, the day after he announced publicly that he was HIV-positive. On the last Queen album released while he was alive, he sang "The Show Must Go On."

Freddie Mercury in a sporty look
on stage at Knebworth, 1986; in an
extravagant stage outfit, ca. 1970; in
a sequined jumpsuit, New York, 1977;
and on stage with leather hotpants
and a towel, Chicago, 1980

JARVIS COCKER

"We just want the right to be different." Pulp

With a name like Jarvis Branson Cocker, and his looks, there are only two possibilities. Either you are a bit of a geek, or a mega pop star hailed by fans as the front man of a whole new style. Jarvis Cocker, the charismatic singer of the British band Pulp, is definitely the latter.

Cocker was born in 1963, the son of a musician in the underground capital of the working class, Sheffield. At the age of fifteen, the eccentric bookworm founded the aforementioned band, though for thirteen years it enjoyed such humble success Cocker had no trouble completing his art studies.

Then, suddenly, in the nineties, when Cocker was already over thirty, came their commercial breakthrough. Britpop was born. At a time when Kurt Cobain ruled the world from the U.S. as the reluctant, stoned king of Grunge, Jarvis Cocker provided a very English counterbalance with his charismatic voice, humorous-cum-ironic intellect, and a virtually inimitable look. Cool Britannia had finally awakened from her Sleeping Beauty slumber.

Cocker's flair for fashion impelled him to make the most of his haggard and defiantly untanned body. The result was often-too-short narrow trousers with wool tank tops that, in terms of taste, could at best be described as neutral. Added to this foundation were double-breasted jackets, skimpy t-shirts, and those atrocious plastic eyeglass frames provided by the UK's National Health Service, which no optician would have dared take out of the drawer before Cocker's appearance. But, amazingly, all these horrors combined into one harmonious image, and led to the surprising realization that nerdy could actually mean sexy.

In 1998, Pulp's last album came out. In retrospect, it marked the high point of Britpop—and its end. Jarvis Cocker currently lives in Paris.

Jarvis Cocker
in British style,
London, 2009

Jarvis Cocker
combines a
cardigan with a
corduroy jacket,
2007

THE
CLASS

MARCELLO MASTROIANNI
GIORGIO ARMANI
HELMUT LANG
HEDI SLIMANE

ICS

MARCELLO MASTROIANNI

Marcello Mastroianni was the face of Italy. Masculine, proud, a little more laid-back than the rest. A film critic once wrote that if Greta Garbo embodied the idea of beauty, then Mastroianni was the embodiment of the man who gazes at that beauty. The Italian actor was not *a* man, he was *all* men at the same time. At the beginning of his career he played the charming lover, later the man in a midlife crisis, and at the end of his life he self-confidently left behind his former sex symbol image. One thing that remained the same during every stage of his life: Mastroianni always looked exactly the way a man ought to.

Even though at first glance he appeared unspectacular, spectacular was never the Italian's style. The actor eschewed flamboyant details, colors, and patterns, and placed the utmost importance on the proper cut. His typically black suits perfectly fit his body, and were combined with classic white shirts with French cuffs and plain black neckties. Mastroianni's only accessories were his legendary smile, his naturally graceful gestures, and above all his innate elegance. He had found his personal uniform, and it was the perfect platform for his masculine charm. The actor proved that an outfit is really only brought to life by the person who wears it. Which was why Mastroianni didn't have to work very hard to become one of Italy's best-dressed men.

Born the son of a cabinetmaker in 1924, Mastroianni, who achieved his greatest fame in the films of Fellini, had a significantly more pragmatic view of himself. For him an actor was nothing more than an "empty box." He certainly knew how to fill it. Over his life he appeared in more than 150 films.

Marcello Mastroianni in a suit jacket with dark sunglasses, a cigarette, and a newspaper in a scene from Federico Fellini's film *8 ½*, 1963

GIORGIO ARMANI

"It's all about good taste."

His recipe for success is really quite simple: "One must have the courage to make one's own decisions. And even to say no once in a while."

"I believe that style is the only real luxury that is really desirable."

That Giorgio Armani has no problem saying no is best demonstrated by his style. Having just started out, the northern Italian designer banned everything from his jackets that until then had been part of a proper gentleman's sport coat. Inner linings, horsehair, interfacings, even the shoulder pads once considered indispensable received no mercy from Armani's scissors. "The suits of those days with their stiff padding looked a bit like armor. Everyone looked the same in them." And one thing Armani didn't want was to look the same as everyone else. Nor did he want a padded suit to provide his posture and stature. For this task is one that the designer, who remains in top physical condition, prefers to do for himself.

"It would be very hard for me to do things somebody else's way."

Everything began very modestly in a Milan department store in the late fifties. After abandoning his medical studies, Armani worked himself up from window dresser to buyer of men's fashion—and was still being told he would "always be the second in command." But one man recognized that Armani's love of unpretentious aesthetics had nothing to do with an unpretentious temperament: Nino Cerruti. The fashion designer made the self-taught Armani responsible for his men's line. A gamble that paid off: "I am sure that with a classical training in tailoring I would never have dared to break so many rules," Armani says today. And he adds that the only fashion training he ever had was from family. "My mother liked muted colors, simple clothes, and masculine-looking jackets. She rejected anything exaggerated." Armani's childhood memories sound like a brief description of his own personal look.

"I've always thought of the t-shirt as the Alpha and Omega of the fashion alphabet,"

And it is precisely this look that, as an independent designer since the early eighties, Giorgio Armani has being marketing throughout the world. The cornerstone of the Armani style—apart from getting rid of the aforementioned excess fabric—is the combination of t-shirts and jackets and the consistent use of non-colors, from beige to dove gray. Only in his women's fashions does the permanently tan designer sometimes cut loose. "My stars," he once said in an interview, "are my dresses." The rest is simple.

Giorgio Armani wears
his typical black in
front of his clothes at
the Giorgio Armani
retrospective, London,
2003

98

HEDI SLIMANE

It happened at some point at the end of the nineties: fashion-conscious men became thin again. No more broad shoulders, goodbye to rippling muscles, away with the broad back. All thanks to the uncompromisingly slender suits designed by Hedi Slimane.

"It's a funny thing about fashion. It really is a very slow medium. It always thinks in phases of only six months, it approaches the world in a very superficial way. But fashion should live entirely in the present, it should be in a position to define the moment."

The son of a Tunisian father and an Italian mother, Slimane was born in Paris in 1968. His mother not only made clothing for the entire family herself, but she also instilled in her son the basic skills of dressmaking. Years later, after studying art history and politics, Slimane became an assistant to his friend, the stylist José Lévy. Then, in 1996, came the sensation: the couture legend Yves Saint Laurent discovered the then-unknown twenty-eight-year-old Slimane and promoted him overnight to chief designer of his men's collection. On one condition—Slimane was to design entirely according to his own personal style. It was a risk that paid off. Within a few years, Slimane (and thus his employers, first YSL and then, from 2000 to 2007, Christian Dior) became the superstar of the fashion industry.

The Frenchman's look was strictly linear, and moved across the color spectrum, without patterns, from black to white, with rare excursions into a bold red. The cut was precise and followed the rules of classic couture. All of Slimane's suits, shirts, drainpipe jeans, and sweaters were so mercilessly tapered and narrow in cut that they did not fit the old male ideal (tall, athletic, muscular). And they did not need to. For Slimane's look only suited men like himself: a new generation of men, artistic, gaunt, intellectual. Fashion was not just a covering of fabric, not merely elegance and style. For Slimane, fashion was the search for the now, the depiction of the imperfect moment. "Everything revolves around this moment of being young, the enormous energy that lies in it, and this idea that anything is possible. This has nothing to do with nostalgia, after all the work is not about me. I am a complete observer here, not someone who is mourning his own youth. That has already been lost, as can be seen." In 2007, Slimane officially retired from the world of fashion.

Hedi Slimane in a slim-cut black suit and scarf at the opening of his exhibition at Galerie Arndt & Partner, Berlin, 2007

On the catwalk in jeans and Chuck Taylors at the end of Dior's 2007 Spring/Summer men's collection show

THE
FASHION
DESIGNE

KARL LAGERFELD
YVES SAINT LAURENT
GIANNI VERSACE
JEAN PAUL GAULTIER
MARTIN MARGIELA
JOHN GALLIANO

RS

*"I am an icy star.
I feel as though
gravity no longer
affects me."*

KARL
LAGERFELD

Karl Lagerfeld is the Sun King Germany never had. Lagerfeld, who speaks what seem like a hundred words a minute in several languages, is a fashion designer (about twenty collections a year for various houses from Chanel to Fendi), a costume designer for films and opera, an interior designer, an illustrator, a photographer, a writer, and a publicist. To top it all off, the German shines with a superb wit, countless *bon mots,* and a seemingly inexhaustible knowledge that, along with his frequently acid tongue, color his numerous interviews. Since 1983, Lagerfeld has confidently directed the creative legacy of Coco Chanel. And he is just as consistent in his own wardrobe choices.

*"I handle myself quite well.
I'm kind of fascist with myself.
There's no discussion.
There is an order. You follow it."*

Over the years, the grandmaster of skilled self-presentation has stylized himself into his own brand, with his white-powdered, unparted, shaving-brush ponytail, dark sunglasses, and nervously fluttering fan. At the beginning of the new millennium he swapped

the fan for fingerless gloves (Lagerfeld dislikes the appearance of his own hands), heavy necklaces (on which, among other things, hang his parents' wedding rings), and stiff, high-neck collars to disguise the signs of aging. The cosmopolitan German's favorite color is black, unpatterned but with a few white highlights. Lagerfeld's greatest coup was to lose more than ninety pounds in a single year as a publicity stunt to fit into the slim-cut Dior suits of his young designer colleague Hedi Slimane. His secret is as straightforward as it is strict. Atypical for the industry, the designer avoids alcohol, tobacco, drugs, and excessive sleep. He no longer he even touches the marmalade toast he once so adored.

The reason for his self-discipline, according to Lagerfeld himself, is his origin. Even if the French long ago adopted him as one of their own (even though he rarely finds a friendly word for his adoptive compatriots), Lagerfeld, born in Hamburg, remains loyal to his Prussian principles.

Karl Lagerfeld in a glittering jacket with leather fingerless gloves and a heavy silver chain at Chanel's 2009 Fall/Winter prêt-à-porter show

In a midnight-blue velvet jacket in front of the Hotel Excelsior, Venice, 2009

Lagerfeld with studded gloves, silver jewelry, and, of course, sunglasses, at Fendi's Spring/Summer women's collection show, Milan, 2009

YVES SAINT LAURENT

Yves Saint Laurent was unquestionably an extremely well-dressed man. But it was a single accessory that made him a style icon: his glasses. It was these dark, square frames that revealed who the wearer really was.

"Dressing is a way of life."

Yves Henri Donat Mathieu Saint Laurent was born in Algeria in 1936. The sensitive boy was particularly close to his mother, a country belle with a passion for everything beautiful. It was she who comforted him when his schoolmates taunted him for his effeminate nature, and her French fashion magazines that allowed him to dream of another, more beautiful world. Saint Laurent began to draw, and at the age of seventeen went to Paris, where he began his career at Dior. As chief designer, he liberated women from the padded waists, bosoms, and shoulders of the time, and with his "trapeze line" became the star of the fashion industry. Despite his success, the young fashion creator was still anxious about his talent and racked by anxiety. His worst nightmare came true when he was

called up for military service in Algeria in 1960, and was replaced at Dior by Marc Bohan. After several nervous breakdowns and electro-shock therapy, the reluctant soldier was given a medical discharge. Though only a short time had passed, Saint Laurent was unable to return to his former position as artistic director. And although, designing under his own name, his most creative period was still to come, Saint Laurent began to calm his anxiety with medication, alcohol, and drugs. The prominent eyeglass frames offered him a certain protection from the outside; the private, timid man was able to hide behind them without sacrificing his aesthetic principles.

"Isn't elegance forgetting what one is wearing?"

In 1971, Saint Laurent allowed himself to be photo-graphed for a perfume ad. The resulting image made him the first pop star of the fashion world. There was the master himself, stark naked—except for his glasses.

Yves Saint Laurent wearing glasses and nothing else in an advertisment, 1971

SAINTLAURENTJEANS

"My dream was always to be a composer, but fashion came very easily."

GIANNI VERSACE

Less is more? You must be joking! Lustrous silk, gold Medusa heads, and eye-catching prints in rich colors—Gianni Versace was anything but a friend of cool understatement. "Why not look audacious? Why not sexy? Why not vulgar? Conventions can be cracked like oysters," the self-confident fashion designer would say to challenge his often unsympathetic critics. And with all the charisma of an Italian star, Versace proved that sometimes less is simply just one thing: less.

"Don't make fashion own you, but you decide what you are, what you want to express by the way you dress and the way to live."

The roots of his opulent look lie deep, at the furthest point of the Italian "boot"—in Reggio di Calabria, where Versace was born in modest circumstances in 1946, the son of a salesman and a dressmaker. After leaving school, he completed a tailoring course, opted to study architecture, and in the end became a fashion designer—first working for others, and, beginning in 1978, under his own name. His designs radiated pure sex and glamour, no less than a declaration of war on the Armani-beige Italian fashion scene.

In the process, Versace gave equal rights to men in fashion, as his wildly patterned men's shirts in lilac, yellow, red, and black silk were no less striking than his designs for women. For Versace, fashion was a living dream of unbridled decadence and ostentatious wealth completely independent of the real world. "Not knowing who you are isn't a crime. Not knowing who you'd like to be—that's where it gets tricky," said the designer when asked to explain his philosophy of life. It is not important who you are—only where you want to go.

For Versace, no detail was too exaggerated, no button too shiny, no artistic trend too far out to be combined together on one piece of fabric that went to the very limits of good taste. The Italian billionaire did not believe in conventions; he believed in himself. "Good taste does not interest me. For me there is no such thing as too much."

"I try to contrast; life today is full of contrast ... We have to change."

In June 1997, Gianni Versace was shot and killed on the steps of his extravagantly refurbished villa Casa Casuarina in Miami Beach.

Gianni Versace
in a glitzy
shirt with gold
ornamentation,
1993

>>
Versace wears
blue jeans with
a gold belt, a
cream shirt, and a
black vest, posing
with a group of
models at his
Spring/Summer
collection, Milan,
1991

JEAN PAUL GAULTIER

A slight penchant for comic provocation? Certainly. A little bit different from the rest? *Bien sûr*. Being difficult to categorize has never represented a problem for Jean Paul Gaultier, the enfant terrible of Parisian haute couture. According to the designer with the bleach-blonde crew cut, fashion should never be taken too seriously.

"Elegance is a question of personality, more than one's clothing."

The very first of Gaultier's fashion shows in 1976 turned classic couture's conventions upside down. Gaultier's former employer, Pierre Cardin, immediately recognized the potential of the collection. After all, his protégé had "challenged the criteria of good taste and bad taste, shocked, troubled, and irritated while enjoying himself clouding the issue with an ambivalent and interchangeable wardrobe." Today, the self-taught Frenchman, born in 1952 the son of an accountant, still avails himself of the styles of different eras for his designs (the best-known of these being Madonna's corset with the conical bra), and is still dismantling clichés with every new collection. And yet he asserts—with a twinkle in his eye—that provocation is the last thing on his mind. All he claims to care

about is the pleasure of playing with fashion. The same goes for his personal wardrobe.

"A man doesn't wear his masculinity on his clothes; his virility is in his head."

Sailor jackets and blue and white striped sweaters are probably the best-known items of his own look. But the fashion creator's personal favorite is the men's skirt. Gaultier has been wearing these airy garments since the mid-eighties, and in so doing has been calling into question gender-specific socialization for far longer than has existed the concept of the "metrosexual."

He himself, of course, sees this in much simpler terms. "A man doesn't wear his masculinity on his clothes; his virility is in his head." In fact, for Gaultier wearing a skirt is almost as enjoyable as "swimming naked." In the end, he has been justified by success. After more than forty years in the fashion business, one thing is clear: this man is no ordinary sailor.

Jean Paul Gaultier in tartan kilt, blue and white striped shirt, and black jacket, 1993; and photographed during the presentation of "La Suite Elle Decoration," Paris, 2010

MARTIN MARGIELA

Martin Margiela is the phantom of the fashion world. The Belgian designer allows no photographs, gives no personal interviews, and on principle never appears in public. This is no less than pure provocation in the personality- driven world of fashion. So how did this invisible man manage to become a style icon? Quite simply with a style that places everything in question, to the extent that the face becomes irrelevant to fashion.

Naturally, very little is known about Margiela. He graduated from the Antwerp Academy of Fine Arts, became a member of the Antwerp Six (the generation of eighties fashion designers that established the Belgian reputation as conceptualists), took his first job as an assistant to Jean Paul Gaultier, founded his own label, Maison Martin Margiela, and, finally, spent a couple of years as chief designer at Hermès. The *New York Times* managed to get hold of a photograph of the chronically reclusive fashion designer. It shows a strikingly attractive face, dark eyes and eyebrows, short hair, and

a facial expression that is *not* amused. That was all—and no more is necessary, for Margiela's style speaks for itself.

Margiela, it seems, is less interested in creating something new than in researching current fashions down to the smallest detail. The Belgian is a fashion anarchist: he openly makes identically cut copies of old designs, sometimes paints his clothes with white wall paint (which peels off while worn, thus showing the age of the piece), prefers to use recycled materials, and takes apart existing garments before reassembling them from their constituent parts (so that the eye can get used to the unconventional new creation). For Margiela, linings, seams, and shoulder pads must abandon their secret existence in favor of visibility, while unhemmed edges and deliberately dangling threads unmask fashion for what it is: the artifice of a beautiful illusion. It is precisely from this that Margiela has withdrawn.

Maison Martin Margiela, 2008/09 Fall/Winter men's collection. A model is wearing an elegant black suit with a fur scarf. The tapered coat is combined with a red scarf and high boots. Margiela makes use of the classic contrast of black and white on a grand scale. White trousers are worn with high black boots and a black suit jacket.

JOHN GALLIANO

The most interesting part of a fashion show is typically over when the last model has left the catwalk, not when the designer responsible for the show enters from the wings to a final round of applause from a persuasive public. Not so with John Galliano. For none of his fabulously staged theme shows would be complete without the master himself. After all, the British designer is one of the most multifaceted personalities in fashion.

"I'm not an artist. Maybe an artist with a small a."

As a boy, Juan Carlos Antonio Galliano Guillén (his given name when born in Gibraltar in 1960) was ceremonially decked out by his Spanish mother on every possible occasion. Although the family lived modestly, it was here that the designer acquired his love of extravagant costume, and as an altar boy at church learned the effect of pomp and ceremonial sensuality. As a result, his student graduation collection, inspired in the eccentric style of French Revolution-era dandies, was a blend of both. Even then he was working in the same manner as he does today: in order to more fully immerse himself in his theme, Galliano sketched his designs in watercolor by candlelight, and he himself began to dress like an *incroyable*.

Both for his collections and his own wardrobe, Galliano—as knowledgeable as he is fearless—time and again dips into the history of art and costume for ideas. Now the creative director at Dior, he has shown himself to be an extravagant quick-change artist. Only his long, often-bleached blond hair, his narrow Errol Flynn beard, and his forever well-toned body survive unchanged to the next season. What remains is a world tour of fashion, one that refuses to reveal its next destination from one day to the next. To date Galliano has played the role of Napoleon, a pirate, and an astronaut, among others. One thing he will surely never be is a chameleon. After all, chameleons survive by passing unnoticed in their surroundings.

John Galliano appears at the 5th Jubilee of CFDA/Vogue Fashion Fund in a sequined suit and a top hat adorned with daisies, New York, 2008

At the Christian Dior 2010 Fall/Winter haute couture show in Paris, contrasting his light beige outfit with a black necktie, black handkerchiefs, and a black hat veil

THE BEAUTI PEOPLE

FUL

THE CARABINIERI

Actually, the Carabinieri are the military police of the Italian armed forces. Their role is to ensure peace and internal security and to defend the Italian borders in emergencies. By definition, the Carabinieri do not belong to an occupational group out for a good time. So looking fabulous as they stroll around the piazzas of Italy in their dashing uniforms is hardly part of their job description. And yet, or so it is said, the Carabinieri are chosen for their height, masculine beauty, and physical presence. Anyone who has spent a mere afternoon in Rome knows this rumor cannot be entirely unfounded.

Since founded in 1854, the members of this Italian special force have worn tailored dark-blue uniforms that have their own special collar patches, rank insignia, and a stylized grenade as their symbol. A broad, bright-red

vertical stripe runs down the side of the pant, stretching the leg and providing visual sophistication. The most significant revamping of the regalia over the years produced the current model, which was reinterpreted by none other than Italian couture legend Valentino, who infused the uniform with an added quotient of elegance.

With so much masculine charm, natural authority, and Italian chic, the motto of the Carabinieri, today 110,000 strong, ensures that no one gets the wrong idea: "Faithful throughout the centuries," or, more succinctly, "Always faithful." At the beginning of the millennium, the highest court of Italy defined exactly what this means: not only untiring service to country, but also faithfulness and exemplary behavior in one's private life. Too good to be true.

Carabinieri patrolling
Rome in tricorne hats and
winter capes; wearing
their summer uniform in
Florence; in full regalia
during a moment's flirtation
outside the Baptistery in
Parma

>>
Carabinieri in the Palazzo
Reale, Naples

On patrol in Venice in
winter uniform

CARY GRANT

"Men want to be him, and women want to meet him." Sean Connery

Cary Grant was undoubtedly one of the best-dressed actors to ever grace the silver screen. No one wore suits with as much panache, charm, and pure elegance. And no one understood Hollywood's rules better than he, for he played a part there his entire life.

In fact, the English actor was named neither Cary nor Grant, nor was he born the well-bred screen gentleman who always cut an impeccable figure in the most awkward of situations. He grew up as Archibald Alexander Leach in a drab working-class neighborhood in Bristol. At fourteen years of age he left school to join a troupe of acrobats. Archibald learned to juggle, dance, and walk on stilts. And in 1920, when he was engaged for a tour of the United States, he grabbed his chance. Leach realized that the movie business demanded more than mere good looks, and without hesitating he changed his name and, above all, his wardrobe.

In choosing clothing, Grant had the courage to opt for simplicity, and was well attuned to what best favored him. His suits were monochrome, dark in the winter and light and summery when the temperature rose. The cut was straightforward, harmonious, unobtrusive, and accentuated only by a casually folded breast-pocket handkerchief. Nothing was to distract attention from his attractive face (his energetic chin with its legendary dimple quickly began to melt women's hearts). Grant's sturdy neck, however, was often hidden behind turned-up collars, and his comparatively large head was brought back into proportion by padded shoulders. It was precisely here that the strength of the Hollywood charmer lay: to recognize faults and transform them into fashion statements.

"When I appear on the screen, I'm playing myself. It's harder to play yourself. I pretend to be a certain kind of man on the screen and I became that man in life. I became me."

Grant retired from the movie business on his own terms at the age of sixty-two. On the screen he had captivated Mae West, Marilyn Monroe, Audrey and Katherine Hepburn, Marlene Dietrich, Grace Kelly, and Ingrid Bergman. In real life, he married five times. His simple reason for his retirement was: "The elegance of the old days is gone."

Cary Grant in a
classic tweed
suit in a scene
from Hitchcock's
Suspicion, 1941

In casual wear,
ca. 1933

>>
Grant sitting
in front of his
painting *Flower
Vendor* by Diego
Rivera, ca. 1955

Leaving his hotel
with an overcoat
and hat, London,
1946

PORFIRIO RUBIROSA

The sparkle of fine champagne, fast cars, an infinite number of women whose beauty was surpassed only by their wealth: that was the life of Porfirio "Rubi" Rubirosa. The Dominican diplomat, a "master in the art of shucking life like an oyster" (as one of his countless bedfellows called him), was born for the good life, which he celebrated daily. His longtime golf partner Frank Sinatra once asked him if he had ever had a full-time job. Rubirosa replied simply: "Women are my profession. Most men want to earn a fortune. I just want to spend a fortune."

Rubirosa's career as a bon vivant began with a scandal. His first official female conquest was Flor de Oro ("golden flower") Trujillo, daughter of the Dominican Republic's dictator, Rafael Trujillo. It was only after the young woman went on a hunger strike that her father reluctantly agreed to let the two marry, only to become an unconditional supporter of his son-in-law long after the two had divorced. Born in 1909, Rubirosa had affairs with Ava Gardner, Zsa Zsa Gabor, Soraya of Iran, and Marilyn Monroe, among others;

and his wives included Doris Duke and Barbara Hutton, the then richest women in the world. He owed his reputation as a "Latin lover" to his sophistication, charm, daring (he was one of the best race-car drivers and polo players of his day), and his good looks. His typical three-piece suits with double-breasted jackets were made from the lightest and finest materials (as was his underwear), his hands were professionally manicured, and his skin silky smooth from the use of honey-based cosmetics. The always-in-shape playboy's discreet jewelry included a pink gold Rolex watch. Another of his trademarks was a single red rose sent to each of his mistresses after a night together. The accompanying card read: "A la mas de las mujeres" (For the most beautiful of women).

In 1965, Rubirosa's life ended as fast as he had lived. After having celebrated a win with his polo team, "Rubi" was driving his Ferrari through the Bois de Boulogne in Paris in the early morning hours when he shot off the road and into a tree. A fitting departure for the last true playboy.

"You have the feeling that this man would break through walls, tear down mountains, and turn the world upside down in order to have you. He is wild, impatient, with a stormy temperament. But when he desires you, he lays his heart at your feet, and he desires you constantly."
Zsa Zsa Gabor

Porfirio Rubirosa in evening dress with bow tie, with his wife Odile Rodin, ca. 1964

Shopping with his wife Odile Rodin, Rubi wears a dark suit and tie, ca. 1956

In polo attire of riding breeches and boots at the Deauville polo field, ca. 1956

TOM FORD

"I would love to change my look, it's just that nothing else suits me.

Tom Ford's style is an attractive balancing act between cool eroticism and intellectual masculinity. When it comes to his image, this handsome American leaves no detail to chance. His suits, typically in dark gray to midnight blue, are made of the finest cloth (more precisely, his own wool-silk and wool-cashmere blends, but often also of velvet), and are precisely tailored for a slender silhouette (the exception being the accentuated shoulders).

"It's about made-to-measure and personality, having something that not everyone has."

His shirts are pristine white, always wrinkle-free, and open to just above the navel. Combined with this are a cool gaze and a neatly trimmed three-day beard, which as accessories usually compete only with a breast-pocket handkerchief and sunglasses ("Sunglasses are like a car on your face: a status symbol"). One thing is clear: Ford is his own favorite muse and his most desirable model. And successfully so—very few master the art of self-presentation as adeptly as this fashion designer with a conspicuous tendency toward perfection.

Ford was born in 1961 in Austin, Texas—not a place known for being particularly chic. His parents, both realtors, placed great value on fine clothing, and on strict rules for wearing it. It was actually a situation seemingly perfect for a fashion-obsessed young man to rebel against in his adolescence. But not for Ford, who as a teenager had rejected rebellion against fabric for aesthetic reasons. At the age of twelve, the boy asked his parents for Gucci loafers. Twenty years later, as creative director of Gucci, he refloated the company from an outdated classic brand to an over-sexualized, must-have label. Since 2003, and his highly publicized separation from the Italian fashion house, Tom Ford has only one focus: Tom Ford. From his own luxury line for men to his debut as a film director, Ford now dedicates himself exclusively to himself and his own aesthetic.

Tom Ford in typical Tom Ford style at the Toronto International Film Festival, 2009

The director in an open shirt and elegant suit at a screening of *A Single Man*. Film Independent, Los Angeles, 2009

JOHNNY DEPP

"I think the thing to do is to enjoy the ride while you're on it."

When one is as improbably handsome as Johnny Depp, everything else seems to follow. For example, he started his career as a TV-series teen idol, and then, within a few years, earned a reputation as a character actor with a marked penchant for being difficult on the set. He has cultivated a Hollywood career despite spending most of the year secluded with his family in a remote village in the south of France. And, above all, he dresses exactly as the mood strikes him.

"My body is my journal, and my tattoos are my story."

John Christopher Depp II, known as Johnny, who by his own account constructs his roles from three components (one-third Lee Strasberg's Method acting, one-third character traits of living persons, and one-third added quirks of his own), proves to be as consistent in the choice of his clothing as he is true to his character. The actor's wardrobe is composed of vibrantly colored well-worn jackets, faded jeans, leather jackets, dark t-shirts, and unironed shirts, often worn with one button too many undone. Depp's style does not differentiate between vintage and designer labels, for it is ultimately the accessories that make the look his own. His unkempt hair, which often looks as if it had not been washed for several days, the bohemian men's jewelry, the glasses and hats are a visual reflection of what Depp really is: a stylistically confident free spirit, a glamorous outsider, a man unafraid to show who he is.

"There's a drive in me that won't allow me to do certain things that are easy."

It is no coincidence that Johnny Depp tends to play offbeat characters in his films. For like his characters, he prefers to stay on the edge, where the boundaries between belonging and exclusion are blurred, where the cultivation of image and its rejection go hand in hand. Like his look, Johnny Depp has maximum recognition value. And he never needed to be marketed like a product.

Johnny Depp
with countless
accessories
including sun-
glasses, bracelets,
necklaces, rings,
a belt chain, and
a bandana, at the
world premiere of
the movie *Pirates
Of The Caribbean:
At World's End*,
Anaheim, 2007

At the *Sweeney
Todd* premiere
with wide-
brimmed hat and
casually draped
scarf, Paris, 2008

"I have come to accept that if I have a new haircut it is front page news."

DAVID BECKHAM

David Beckham is the original metrosexual. Why? Before him, the word simply did not exist. There was no need for it. Before Beckham, no one had ever blurred the boundaries between the sexes without moving even an inch away from testosterone-laden masculinity.

"The spotlight will always be on me, but it's something I'm learning to live with as the years go by."

Of course, Beckham is first and foremost a footballer. Born in 1975, the Englishman inherited from his hairdresser mother and kitchen fitter father a passion for Manchester United football—the talent to become the star of the team was his own doing. His specialties of impeccable passing and unforgivingly accurate free kicks quickly had competition for the attention of his global community of fans: his personal style. Beckham the ambitious player became the Beckham of today—the English athlete's star power made him an image-maker, a role model, and a style icon.

From the beginning, Beckham has made dual use of the football field—as a sporting arena to win every imaginable title, and as a global stage where he narcissistically presents his perfectly modeled body, his hairstyles that change with the seasons (from blond spikes to completely bald to a high-set ponytail), and his accessories, perfectly lit under the floodlights. David Beckham has succeeded in doing what no had ever done before—to break down the traditional male image without sacrificing any of his masculinity. The result is the metrosexual man, who seems to float above all the gender-based rules of style and behavior.

Today, David Beckham, twice named "World Footballer of the Year," is seldom in the headlines for his athletic feats. Alongside his wife Victoria, he is now one of the world's most lucrative media stars. And he probably does not need to worry about a career after leaving the world of sport.

David Beckham in a sporty
style at Adidas Originals by
Originals, Milan, 2010

In a shiny dark suit with
loosely buttoned shirt and
breast-pocket handkerchief
to celebrate the opening of
the David Beckham Academy,
Beverly Hills, 2005

THE
BAND

THE BEATLES
THE SEX PISTOLS
RUN–D.M.C.

S

THE BEATLES

That the look of a band is at least as important as the music was something Brian Epstein picked up on early. In 1961, the English music entrepreneur signed a young Liverpool band that had until then played mainly in dubious Hamburg clubs, drinking heavily and without set lists, wearing shabby fifties leather outfits. Not with Epstein.

"We saw a guy in Hamburg whose hair we liked. John and I were hitchhiking to Paris. We asked him to cut our hair like he cut his."

For their planned English breakthrough he made his protégés wear custom-made Chelsea boots and narrow black suits, imposed a suitable stage presence, and insisted on a fixed performance repertoire. The band members were permitted to keep, as a memento of their time in Hamburg, only their soon-to-be famous mop-top haircuts, which they had copied from the German artist Jürgen Vollmer. And although the group's debut in the south of England took place in front of an audience of just eighteen people, Epstein was right. For the band was none other than the Beatles.

"They glanced at my hair and said, Yes, we want that funny haircut too."

Beginning in the early sixties, their look went around the world as fast as their songs. And John Lennon, Paul McCartney, George Harrison, and Ringo Starr knew how to deal with it. What today is perceived as calculated music marketing (reinventing oneself with every new recording), was simple intuition for the members of the Beatles. The black suits were soon replaced by pastel-colored collarless suits in the Edwardian "teddy-boy" style that had been adopted with particular enthusiasm by the young Mods in mid-sixties England. From 1967, Lennon, McCartney, Harrison, and Starr still appeared in matching clothing, but they were happy to try out new looks: reflecting the spirit of the times, they took to rich colors, turtlenecks, paisley patterns, flower prints, and later to Indian-inspired hippie outfits. With each subsequent album, the Beatles' look grew less formal and more a reflection of the individual members' personalities. The harmonious boy band with their bold fashion statements had become a grown-up group of four creative individuals. The year 1970 witnessed the release of the last album the "world sensation from Liverpool" would record together.

The Beatles in their mop tops and matching dark suits after being awarded the MBE (Member of the Order of the British Empire) by the Queen, 1965

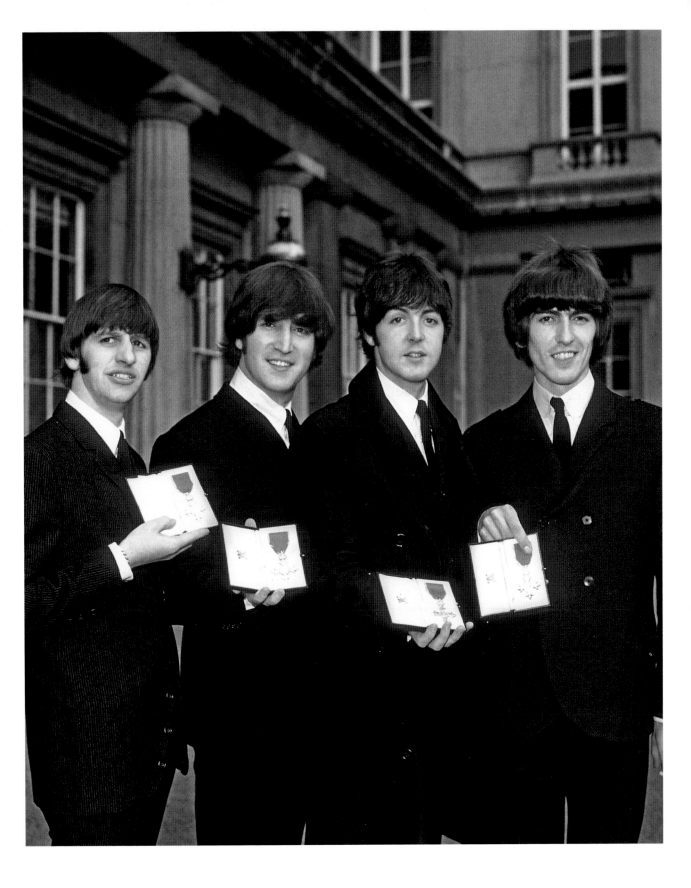

The Beatles in collarless suits, ca. 1964

John Lennon wears a sporran for the presentation of the album *Sergeant Pepper's Lonely Hearts Club Band*, London, 1967

THE SEX PISTOLS

*"The Pistols were like my work of art.
They were my canvas."*
Malcolm McLaren

Seventies Great Britain was not exactly a place to have fun. Those who weren't surfing along on the glamorous spangled disco wave probably had little to expect from life apart from drab apartment blocks, unemployment, limited educational opportunities, and, above all, the deadly boredom of the bourgeoisie. The stuffy England of the seventies had nothing to offer its youngsters. What ever did become of the "No Future" kids? They would create the first anti-establishment movement to lastingly shake up the nation. Subversive violence and an aggressive street attitude were the trademarks of the first punk generation. Its leaders were four young lads who, with their powerful riffs and disheveled looks, perfectly captured their abandoned generation's state of mind.

*"I'll die before I'm 25,
and when I do I'll
have lived the way
I wanted to."*
Sid Vicious

Malcolm McLaren,
Vivienne Westwood's
partner at the time,
became the manager of the

Sex Pistols in 1975. The first addition to the band was John Lydon, who, with his poor dental hygiene, became known as Johnny Rotten. Sid Vicious (originally John Simon Ritchie) joined them some two years later, when the band of amateur musicians had already achieved their first hit, "Anarchy in the UK." The song became a punk classic, as did their look, masterminded by Vivienne Westwood: safety pins in their ears, spiked hair, torn tight pants, military boots, distressed clothes (remodeled with the use of, among other things, feathers, zippers, rivets, chains, and chicken bones) and t-shirts with offensive motifs (from a desecrated Union Jack to a Queen with piercings, every taboo was broken for maximum shock value).

*"I'm not chic, I could
never be chic."* *Sid Vicious*

The early Eighties saw the end of anarchy. Sid Vicious succumbed to his heroin addiction in 1977, and the other band members were forced to watch as the aesthetic of the underground became socially acceptable mainstream chic.

*"I always feel more comfortable in chaotic surroundings.
I don't know why that is. I think order is dull. There is
something about this kind of desire for order, particularly in
Anglo-Saxon cultures, that drive out this ability for the
streets to become a really exotic, amorphous, chaotic, organic
place where ideas can, basically, develop."* Malcolm McLaren

*"Sometimes the most positive thing you can be in a
boring society is absolutely negative."* Johnny Rotten

Album cover for *God Save The Queen*
by the Sex Pistols, released in 1977

In front of their tour bus in scruffy
stage clothes, 1978

RUN-D.M.C.

"You really need to be on the edge and you have to keep your eyes open." Jam Master Jay

They were the first rappers featured on the cover of *Rolling Stone,* the first to have records reach gold, platinum, and even double-platinum status, the first to have their videos on MTV. Run-D.M.C. was not simply a group of three talented musicians. Run-D.M.C. were rap pioneers. In the early eighties their spectacular hard beats and lyrics created a revolution in American pop culture. And their look? They quite simply popularized a completely new style of fashion.

"How I dressed in high school is the way we dressed." Jam Master Jay

It all began in the New York borough of Queens. In 1982, Jason "Jam Master Jay" Mizell, Joseph "Run" Simmons, and Darryl "D.M.C." McDaniels ("D.M.C." stood for "Dirty, Mostly Clean") founded the rap group distinguished by their raw beats and aggressive texts, and the combination, completely new at the time, of hip-hop and rock music. Success was not long in coming, and their second single was their commercial

breakthrough—with the result that suddenly not only was everyone listening to Run-D.M.C., but they all wanted to look as cool as the New York group. For contrary to the dress codes of the rap veterans of the time, such as Afrika Bambaataa and Melle Mel of Grandmaster Flash and the Furious Five, with an obvious allegiance to the disco look of skintight leather pants and rhinestone-studded shirts, the members of Run-D.M.C. took the street as a stylistic model. With phat black pants, phat black jackets, phat gold chains, and Adidas Superstars worn without laces, the three MCs were aesthetic heavyweights in the previously fanciful world of fashion.

In 2002, Jam Master Jay was shot and killed by an unknown assailant in a New York recording studio. His tribute to his favorite shoes in the song "My Adidas" is unforgettable: "Got blue and black, when it's time to chill / And yellow and green, when it's time to get ill."

"My Adidas walked through concert doors and roamed all over coliseum floors."
Run-D.M.C.

Run-D.M.C. with heavy gold chains, 1988

The group in Adidas style, 1986

>>
Jam Master Jay, D.M.C., and DJ Run in Kangol hats and bomber jackets, a popular look of the 1980s

THE EXTRA-TERREST

ELVIS PRESLEY
ZIGGY STARDUST
BOOTSY COLLINS
MICHAEL JACKSON
BOY GEORGE

RIALS

ELVIS PRESLEY

"I'm not trying to be sexy. It's just my way of expressing myself when I move around."

He was the King. Of music, of pelvic gyrations, and of breaking down barriers. Or, as Leonard Bernstein aptly put it, "Elvis is the greatest cultural force in the twentieth century. He introduced the beat to everything, music, language, clothes." If success is measured in sales, Elvis Presley is the most successful artist of all time.

Presley's style went hand in hand with his sound—both were an often provocative blend of different cultures, and both continued to develop over the length of his ca-   reer.
His music was a blend of   "white"
country, "black" rhythm and   blues, and
gospel unprecedented until his   emergence
in the 1950s. His wardrobe was the same. At the start of his career, Presley combined the look of the white and black working classes of the American South. His hair—dyed deep black and heavily pomaded—and matching sideburns were the same sported by white truck drivers (which he was for a time), and he bought his clothes in African-American stores such as Lansky's in Memphis. When Presley showed up to record his first hit he was wearing a white, lacy shirt, pink pants with black piping, and white bucks.

In the sixties, when every teenager had already fallen under the spell of his prohibited stage gyrations, Presley

modified his style, preferring unpretentious suits and stiffly sculpted hair. But it was not long before the King showed his real greatness. At his dazzling 1968 comeback concert, after his military service and taking some personal time, Presley stepped into the limelight in a skin-tight black leather suit. There was no going back. Beginning in the seventies Presley made his frenzied appearances on stage in fabulous, glitzy costumes, preferably in white and gold, often adorned with brocade trim. His capes and jackets were notorious for their monumental glitz and exaggeratedly high collars, his gold jewelry for its incredible weight. Yet in spite of all the theatrics, the simple cut of his jumpsuits was patterned on the overalls of a regular workingman, whom Presley, never forgetting his humble origins, identified with until the end.

Incidentally, Presley wore the complete legendary gold lame suit only once on stage. The outfit had been made from real gold leaf, and at the time was worth more than $10,000. When Presley fell to his knees during the performance, his manager had to ask him to stop. After all, he left $50 worth of gold dust sprinkled on the stage.

Elvis Presley dancing in a stylized prison uniform during a publicity shoot for the movie *Jailhouse Rock*, 1957; on stage in a white jumpsuit with color appliqué, 1972; in the movie *Love Me Tender* with a brown velvet jacket, Los Angeles, 1956; and in the gold lame suit created by Nudie Cohen, 1957

Sincerely Your Elvis

"When I was a boy, I always saw myself as a hero in comic books and in movies. I grew up believing this dream."

Elvis Presley in a white shirt and tie backstage at an appearance in Jacksonville, 1956

On stage in a white jumpsuit with glitter appliqué, 1974

ZIGGY STARDUST

"Call me Ziggy, call me Ziggy Stardust!" David Bowie

He was the first musician to slip into a different identity onstage. In 1972, David Bowie not only sang about Ziggy Stardust, he was Ziggy Stardust. An androgynous creature fallen from heaven, who had come to earth to warn humanity against the inevitable end of the world—and who finally succumbed to earthly temptations, mutated into a rock superstar, and found his own inevitable end by being torn to pieces by his fanatical fans. Bowie's alter ego was nothing more than an uninhibited mix of biblical motifs and the correct dose of sex, drugs, and rock 'n' roll. The music to the story became a milestone of rock history—and with it the outfits of Ziggy Stardust, the superego of glam rock.

"I'm the last person to pretend that I'm a radio. I'd rather go out and be a color television set."

A dangerous crew cut in glowing orange and red, a face painted in iridescent pure white and bold colors, and a stick-thin body clothed in extremely skin-tight shimmering suits with spangled stripes—this was the look of the space narcissist. Outfits that looked just like costumes on other men, for Ziggy Stardust were perfectly natural. The designs by Freddie Burretti (also known as Rudi Valentino), Natasha Korniloff, and above all Kansai Yamamoto, had one thing in common: they seemed to be cut from an unknown, prismatically glittering space fabric—just right for the superstar who was simply not of this world. The look was completed by what was probably history's first and only cool mullet (short in the front, long in the back), created by London hairdresser Suzy Fussey, and which became as popular as Lady Diana's hairstyle a decade later (with the difference that Ziggy Stardust's style could be worn by either sex). Pierre La Roche was responsible for the makeup, consisting mainly of white Japanese rice powder, black Indian kohl pencil, and ethereally glowing waves of color (often in tones of pink and mauve).

"When you've had red hair and no eyebrows you've got to have a sense of humor!"

As great as Ziggy Stardust's success, was his rapid and unexpected end: on July 3, 1973, at a concert at London's Hammersmith Odeon, David Bowie appeared on stage for the last time as the interstellar rock star.

*"I was the
Space Invader."*
David Bowie

David Bowie as Ziggy
Stardust, wearing a
spaceman costume
with platform shoes,
ca. 1970

In a Ziggy Stardust
outfit with carrot-red
hair and flame-
patterned suit, ca.
1973

BOOTSY COLLINS

Those believing Elton John wears the most outlandish glasses in show business are not just mistaken; they have not had the good fortune of having seen the spectacular Bootsy Collins. This American funk bassist not only drops a funky groove, he lives on one. Above all visually.

His start in show business was phenomenal from a musical standpoint, though rather modest as his attire was concerned. In 1969, James Brown hired seventeen-year-old William "Bootsy" Collins and his band the Pacemakers to back him up. Brown soon became a father figure for Collins, controlling everything from his bedtime to his wardrobe. In spite of worldwide successes such as "Sex Machine" and "Talkin' Loud And Sayin' Nothing," after only two years Brown's pupil finally did what most young men with strict fathers do: he rebelled.

Collins left the band. The result was a new sound (deep, bubbling, and driving), a new life (without any rules or regulations), and above all a new look. Collins dabbled with the style of glam-rock, and its wow factor and glitzy glamour became the basis of the Bootsy style. His next group, Bootsy's Rubber Band, did their name justice. Today, with his new star-shaped, rhinestone-encrusted bass, the "Space Bass" (built today by Manuel Salvador of Guitar Craft), the musician still lets the beat float and expand like a rubber band. The wardrobe accompanying his sound includes oversize top hats, star-shaped sunglasses, skin-tight shorts, bell-bottoms, and ultra-tall platform boots in bright fluorescent colors. All in one look, all worn by one man, and all guaranteed to be encrusted with rhinestones.

In 2010, Collins founded the Funk University, an online school for bass guitarists. Seminars on clothing are not part of the curriculum—not surprisingly, for Collins' style is inimitable.

Bootsy Collins in a mustard-yellow
suit and platform shoes, 1990s

Bootsy playing his space bass in a
sequined outfit, New York, 1996

In full regalia, with star sunglasses
and star-shaped bass, ca. 1970

MICHAEL JACKSON

It all began quite innocently. Five nice boys in nice outfits, who, to everyone's delight, even sang really nice songs. Despite their huge success, and as charming as the Jackson 5 appeared on stage in the late sixties, its members couldn't manage to become truly global stars. One of the brothers sensed the need for change: Michael Jackson, later known as the King of Pop.

> *"I'm never pleased with anything, I'm a perfectionist, it's part of who I am."*

His breakthrough as a solo artist came with the album *Off the Wall*. There was Michael Jackson, still wearing a conservative black tuxedo with a gleaming white shirt, but already with glimmering white socks. This ensemble was the perfect visualization of his sound: old-school rhythm and blues with clear disco influences. His next album, *Thriller*, turned it up a notch: the white suit, black open-necked shirt, and gold breast-pocket handkerchief only hinted at the sensation soon to come.

In 1983, on a television special commemorating the 25th anniversary of the Motown label (on which the Jackson 5 appeared), Michael Jackson performed "Billie Jean." His outfit consisted of a black sequined jacket, a silver shirt, white socks under shortened pants, a black hat, and a white sequined glove. Not two gloves, just one. Jackson performed the moonwalk for the first time and unmistakably grabbed his crotch with that spot-lit sequined hand. That did it. *Thriller* became the bestselling album of all time.

For years the single glove remained Jacko's trademark, even when the dark sequined jacket gave way to garish ringmaster costumes and gold lamé jumpsuits. In retrospect, the accessory represented the start of the pop star's race for his own ever-evolving image. It was a race Michael Jackson couldn't win.

Michael Jackson in his legendary outfit for his appearance on *Motown: Yesterday, Today, Forever*, 1983

>>

With gold shin guards and an arm brace as accessories to his flowing silk shirt, on stage at the benefit concert *A Night at the Apollo*, New York, 2002

The King of Pop with leather straps and studded belt singing at the Capital Centre, Landover, 1988

"With the way I look, I'm protected from getting stuck in lousy jobs."

BOY GEORGE

"I can do anything. In GQ, I appeared as a man."

Those who listened to New Wave in the eighties were sure to have had a Culture Club album on their shelf. But it was not the catchy, radio-friendly pop-soul sound that made the British band so hugely successful. Their meteoric rise was due to one thing: a charismatic front man, a gently smiling creature who drew attention with brightly colored makeup and a passion for dressing up. His name was Boy George.

"I knew style and content went hand in hand."

It all began in front of the television, for that was where twelve-year-old George O'Dowd, the son of Irish Catholic immigrants, first saw the androgynous pop star David Bowie. "Terrible," his grandmother declared. "So beautiful," thought George. By then it was clear to the boy that the humdrum rules and obligations of bourgeois life with were not for him. Expelled from school, the teenager immedi-

ately fled to London, and George O'Dowd became Boy George. And he created a new look to go with his new identity. Garishly done up, with a passion for clothes and extreme chic, as a "Blitz Kid" and a New Romantic he defied the boring strictures of the everyday and became a celebrity on the London nightlife scene. "As long as I was getting caught up in the flashbulbs every evening, I had a reason to get up the next day and think up a new costume." Boy George's stage was the dance floor, long before he wrote his first song. It was only with the founding of Culture Club and its rapid success that the whole world became a stage on which to dance.

"I'm always being inspired."

Since his giddy rise to fame in 1982, the singer, now also a DJ, has passed through nearly every stage of a pop star's life, including failures, scandals, and run-ins with the law. But one quality has never abandoned the musician—the courage to stand up for himself.

Boy George with dreadlocks and a headscarf under a black hat, 1981

Culture Club's singer wearing a white coat with black seams and decorative patches, 1987

BIOGRA

PHIES

GIANNI AGNELLI was born in 1921 in Turin, Italy, where he died in 2003. He was the grandson of Giovanni Agnelli senior, the founder of the Italian car manufacturer Fiat. After his military service he lived a playboy's life until 1953, when he became the vice president of Fiat. He married and had two children. Because he had a law degree Agnelli was given the nickname "L'Avvocato" (the lawyer). One of the most important figures in Italy's economy, he was a symbol of Italian capitalism and regarded by many as the true "king of Italy."

GIORGIO ARMANI was born in 1934 in Piacenza, Italy. After abandoning his medical studies he worked as a window dresser and fashion buyer. From 1961 to 1970 he worked for Nino Cerruti's men's fashion line, Hitman. Since 1975 he has been working under the name Giorgio Armani S.p.A. His company grew rapidly, and Armani distinguished himself as a good businessman. He works in Milan and owns a house on the Italian Mediterranean island of Pantelleria. Since the death of his business and life partner Sergio Galeotti in 1985, he has lived alone.

FRED ASTAIRE was born Frederick Austerlitz in 1899 in Omaha, Nebraska, and died in 1987 in Los Angeles. As a child he attended dance class with his sister, and from 1917 to 1932 they appeared together on Broadway. In 1933 he played his first leading role in a movie in *Flying Down to Rio*. From then on this virtuoso dancer and choreographer helped shape the movie musical genre. He married twice and had three children.

THE BEATLES were a British pop-rock band from 1960 to 1970 composed of John Lennon, Paul McCartney, George Harrison, and Ringo Starr. The group is considered the first boy band and was among the most commercially successful bands of the twentieth century. After their early years in Hamburg, their big break came in 1963 with an appearance on the popular Associated Television (ATV) program *Sunday Night at the London Palladium*, which had 15 million viewers. With their rising popularity, the ecstatic and increasingly uncontrollable hysteria of their female fans also grew, becoming known as Beatlemania. With their music and films they had a lasting influence on pop culture and contributed to the development of the music video.

DAVID BECKHAM was born David Robert Joseph Beckham in 1975, in Leytonstone, London. He began his professional career as a footballer with Manchester United in 1992 and became the team's most important player. From November 2000 to July 2006 he was captain of England's national team. His physical appearance made him the prototype of the metrosexual man, an image he markets in advertising, including for cosmetics. In 1999 he married Victoria Adams, with whom he has three sons. They live in Los Angeles.

ANDRÉ BENJAMIN was born André Lauren Benjamin in Atlanta, Georgia, in 1975, and he works under various pseudonyms, the most popular being André 3000. With his schoolmate Big Boi he formed the band Outkast. In 1994 they released their first album, and have since then received high critical praise. Since 2005 Benjamin has also taken up acting. His extravagant, attention-getting style has now found expression in his own fashion line, on which he is currently working.

JAMES BOND, also known as 007, is a fictional agent for the British secret service, MI6. Created by the writer Ian Fleming in 1952, he became world-famous in the 1960s through the successful film franchise, and to date has been interpreted by Sean Connery, George Lazenby, Roger Moore, Timothy Dalton, Pierce Brosnan, and Daniel Craig. Today the figure of James Bond is a pop culture icon.

DAVID BOWIE was born Robert Jones in London in 1947. **ZIGGY STARDUST** was a personality created and presented by him in the 1972 concept album *The Rise and Fall of Ziggy Stardust and the Spiders from Mars*. The album tells the story of Ziggy Stardust, symbolic of the sexually promiscuous, drug-abusing rock star, a role for which David Bowie appeared in spectacular clothing and androgynous make-up. In 1973 he announced the end of the Ziggy Stardust era.

MARLON BRANDO was born in 1924 in Omaha, Nebraska, and died in 2004 in Los Angeles. He was one of the best and highest-paid character actors in Hollywood. He became the idol of rebellious youth in 1954 with his film *The Wild Ones*. In 1971 he had his most popular role as Vito Corleone in *The Godfather*. The film became part of movie history and earned him an Oscar. He was married four times and fathered seven children.

TRUMAN CAPOTE was born Truman Streckfus Persons in 1924 in New Orleans and died in 1984 in Los Angeles. In 1942 he took a job as an editorial assistant at the *New Yorker*. In 1945 he received the prestigious O. Henry Award for his short stories, and was considered an exceptionally talented literary figure. His commercial breakthrough came with *Breakfast at Tiffany's*, and his true crime book *In Cold Blood* became a bestseller in 1966. With this non-fiction book he founded a new genre: New Journalism. A planned roman à clef about the secrets of high society led to his being shunned by his social circles. His drug and alcohol addictions dramatically worsened. In his last years he suffered from depression and died a lonely death from an overdose of pills.

THE CARABINIERI (Arma dei Carabinieri) are an Italian police force founded by Vittorio Emanuele I, King of Sardinia, in 1814. A branch of the army, it had military as well as police duties. Since 2000 it is an independent part of the Italian armed forces, alongside the army, navy, and air force. Organizationally, the Carabinieri are part of the ministry of defense, under whose budget they appear.

JOHNNY CASH was born in 1932 in Kingsland, Arkansas, and died in 2003 in Nashville, Tennessee. In August 1955 he made his first major appearance supporting Elvis Presley. His distinctive bass-baritone voice and the characteristic "boom-chicka-boom" sound of his backing band the Tennessee Three made him famous. As the "Man in Black" he became a legend in his own lifetime in both country and folk music. After getting off drugs, he finally married June Carter, his second wife and the great love of his life.

GEORGE CLOONEY was born in 1961 in Lexington, Kentucky, the son of a news anchorman, which brought him into contact with television at an early age . After several less successful roles, in the mid-nineties he reached international fame as a doctor in the hospital series *ER*. His first cinematic success was the Tarantino film *From Dusk Till Dawn*, which attained cult status. In addition to acting, Clooney is a screenwriter, producer, and director, and is also involved in politics. He owns a villa on Lake Como in Italy.

KURT COBAIN was born in 1967 in Aberdeen, Washington, and died in 1994 in Seattle. The singer, songwriter, and guitarist became famous worldwide with the grunge band Nirvana (1987 to 1994) and he became the image and voice of Generation X. The band's big break came in 1991 with the single "Smells Like Teen Spirit" and the album *Nevermind*. The drug-addicted musician suffered from severe psychological problems, which ultimately led to him taking his own life.

JARVIS COCKER was born in 1963 in Sheffield, England. The musician because famous as the frontman of the Britpop band Pulp, which he founded with friends in the late 70s, and whose lineup frequently changed. The last Pulp recording was released in 2002, and his first solo album in 2006. The celebrity hype became too much for him and he moved to France, and he now lives in Paris with his wife and son.

BOOTSY COLLINS was born William Collins in 1951 in Cincinnati, Ohio. He had has big break in 1969 when James Brown hired him and his band the Pacemakers. His groovy bass-playing and extravagant outfits have made him famous, or infamous, worldwide. He is considered one of the most important funk musicians of all time. Since breaking with James Brown in 1971 he has worked on various solo projects, including excursions into other musical genres.

JAMES DEAN was born in 1931 in Marion, Indiana, and died in 1955 near Cholame, California, in a car accident. In 1954 he signed his first Hollywood contract for his first film, *East of Eden*, a role that brought him widespread fame as a character actor. As the sensitive *Rebel Without a Cause* he became a role model for the wild youth of puritanical America. He is considered one of the greatest film stars of all time.

JOHNNY DEPP was born in 1963 in Owensboro, Kentucky. He became an international teen idol in 1987 with the TV series 21 *Jump Street*. His break in film came in 1990 with *Edward Scissorhands*, which became a showpiece for his acting talent and gave him a greater choice of roles. He has a preference for somewhat offbeat but sensitive characters, and his long-standing friendship with director Tim Burton has produced numerous collaborations. He lives with his girlfriend and their two children in the south of France.

LAPO ELKANN was born in 1977 in New York, the grandson of the Fiat businessman Gianni Agnelli, and was raised in France. He studied international relations and in 2004 took over the marketing of Fiat, whose image he revamped. After withdrawing from the public eye for a year because of drug abuse, he made a comeback in 2006. He founded his own fashion label, Italia Independent, and the communications firm Independent Ideas. He returned to Fiat in 2007 and since 2010 is the president of the Fiat Group's board of directors.

FALCO was born in 1957 in Vienna as Johann Hölzel and died in a car accident in 1998 near Puerto Plata, Dominican Republic. After his first musical experiences in various bands in the late seventies he began a solo career with the name Falco. The Austrian singer and composer had has big break in 1982 with the single "Der Kommissar." From then on he had a lasting influence on German-language music, and he also became popular internationally. In 1985 his successful single "Rock Me Amadeus" made him the first German-speaking artist to top the U.S. charts. He retired to the Dominican Republic in 1996.

BRYAN FERRY was born in 1945 in Washington, England. He became known in the 1970s as the singer of the band Roxy Music, then representatives of the glam rock scene. Since 1973 he has also had a successful solo career, above all with covers versions of rock, pop, and jazz classics of the 1930s. He has been married once and has four sons.

TOM FORD was born in 1961 in Austin, Texas. He first studied art history at the University of New York, but then concentrated on architecture at the Parsons School of Design in New York and Paris. He began working for Gucci beginning in 1990, and became its creative director in 1992, reviving the battered image of the traditional Italian label. After the Gucci Group took over the Yves Saint Laurent label, he also became responsible for their designs. Finally, in 2003 he founded his own fashion label, Tom Ford, concentrating on men's fashion and accessories. In 2009 he debuted as a film director with *A Single Man*.

JOHN GALLIANO was born in 1960 in British Gibraltar as Juan Carlos Antonio Galliano. As a child he moved to London, where he graduated from the St. Martin's School of Art and Design in 1984. His big break as a couturier came in 1995 designing for Givenchy, and he moved to Christian Dior a year later. This extravagant fashion designer's trademarks are lavishly presented shows and historically inspired designs mixed with modern influences. The British designer's main residence is in Paris.

JEAN PAUL GAULTIER was born in Paris in 1952. In 1970 he started work as an assistant to the French fashion designer Pierre Cardin. At the age of twenty-four he started his own label, which has since expanded internationally. In terms of style he proved to be a revolutionary even in his early years. Because of this, and because of his unorthodox fashion shows, he is considered an eccentric and provocateur among fashion designers.

BOY GEORGE was born in 1961 as George Alan O'Dowd in Bexleyheath, London. The British singer became a world-wide pop idol as the dazzling frontman of the New Wave band Culture Club. When the band broke up in 1987, he began a solo career and, since the nineties, has also worked as a D.J. A gay icon, his turbulent private life has been marred by scandal.

CARY GRANT was born in 1904 in Bristol, England, as Alexander Archibald Leach, and died in 1986 in Los Angeles. In 1932 he signed a five-year contract with Paramount Pictures, where he began to sow the seeds of his fame. Between 1930 and 1960 he was among the most versatile and internationally successful actors, and his projects with his friend the director Alfred Hitchcock form part of cinematic history. He retired from the movie business in 1966. He married five times in all, and had one daughter.

CHE GUEVARA was born Ernesto Guevara de la Serna in 1928 in Rosario, Argentina, and was executed in 1967 in Higueras, Bolivia. After studying medicine, in 1954 he joined forces with the exiled Cuban revolutionary Fidel Castro in Mexico. After the Cuban revolution (1956–59), in which he played a leading role, he became a symbolic figure and participated in the Cuban government. In 1964 he left his government post and attempted, in vain, to export the Cuban revolution model to other countries. He is a national hero in Cuba, and his death converted him into a revered martyr of left-wing independence and freedom movements throughout the world.

JIMI HENDRIX, actually James Marshall Hendrix, was born in 1942 in Seattle, Washington, and died in 1970 under mysterious circumstances at the age of twenty-seven in London. He was one of the greatest guitar virtuosos in musical history, and had a lasting influence on the role of the electric guitar in rock music. His sensational live appearances became cult events, and his appearance at Woodstock became legendary for his incendiary version of "The Star-Spangled Banner."

MICHAEL JACKSON was born in 1958 in Gary, Indiana, and died in 2009 in Los Angeles. The singer, songwriter, and dancer was one of the most successful musicians and entertainers of our time, and came to be known as the King of Pop. By the age of five he was a star alongside his brothers in the Jackson Five. With his solo album *Thriller* (1982), still the highest-selling album in musical history, Michael Jackson became the complete megastar. Ultimately, his musical triumphs were overshadowed by private scandals: he repeatedly underwent plastic surgery and was taken to court several times for, among other charges, child abuse. He married twice and had three children.

MICK JAGGER was born in 1943 in Dartford, Kent, England. The British singer and rock musician, co-founder and frontman of the Rolling Stones, has been since the sixties one of the world's most popular musicians. The band had its first worldwide hit in 1965 with the song "I Can't Get No Satisfaction." Besides music, Jagger has frequently acted in films. In 2003 he received a British knighthood for his services to popular music. He has married twice and has had countless affairs. So far he has seven children and two grandchildren.

JOHN F. KENNEDY was born John Fitzgerald Kennedy in 1917 in Brookline, Massachusetts, and was assassinated in 1963 in Dallas, Texas. At forty-three years of age he became the youngest president of the United States. In spite of his brief presidency, he was one of the most influential U.S. presidents and became a symbol of a new start and a more humane future. His death remains shrouded in mystery.

KARL LAGERFELD was born in 1933 in Hamburg. From 1954 to 1957 he trained as a couturier while working for the French designer Pierre Balmain. In 1958 he became an independent designer and worked for Jean Patou, Chloé, Coco Chanel, Fendi, and his own label Karl Lagerfeld Impression. With his striking creations he became a leading figure on the international fashion and design scene. In 1987 he turned to photography and began designing costumes for the theater. He has homes in Paris, Monaco, and Biarritz.

HELMUT LANG was born in 1956 in Vienna, where he opened his first fashion boutique at the age of twenty-three. In 1986 he founded a fashion label under his own name. His international break came in the early nineties with his minimalist creations in high-tech fabrics. In 2005 he sold his label and retired from the fashion world. He now lives in a house on Long Island, near New York City, where he focuses on his art.

RALPH LAUREN was born Ralph Lifshitz in 1939 in the Bronx, New York. After serving in the military from 1962 to 1964 he worked as a salesman for the traditional men's clothier Brooks Brothers. In 1967 he obtained from Brooks the rights to the Polo label, whose logo is a small embroidered polo player. He struck out on his own and designed his first men's collection. In 1964 he married Ricky Low-Beer, with whom he has three children. In 1997 Polo Ralph Lauren Inc. became the largest incorporated fashion company in the United States. He lives in Bedford, Connecticut.

MARTIN MARGIELA was born in 1957 in Louvain, Belgium. He studied at the Antwerp Royal Academy of Fine Arts and formed part of the Antwerp Six, a generation of fashion designers that established the Belgian reputation as conceptualists. He worked as an assistant to Jean Paul Gaultier and beginning in 1998 as head designer at Hermès. The label of Maison Martin Margiela, which he founded in 1988, now belongs to the Diesel group.

MARCELLO MASTROIANNI was born in 1924 in Fontana Liri, Italy, and died in 1996 in Paris. In 1945, he began his acting career principally on the stage, where Luchino Visconti discovered him, and from 1948 worked increasingly in roles in postwar Italian neorealist cinema. He made his breakthrough in 1959 with *La dolce vita*. In the 1960s he became one of the busiest European actors and reached global stardom under the frequent direction of Federico Fellini. His marriage was overshadowed by affairs, and he was the father of two daughters.

STEVE MCQUEEN was born in 1930 in Indianapolis and died in Mexico in 1980 of lung cancer. After a difficult childhood he joined the Marine Corps at the age of seventeen. In 1956, after studying drama in New York, he played his first role on Broadway. Following Marlon Brando and James Dean, he was the prototypical anti-hero of sixties and seventies film. His great passion from his early years was motor sports, and he often did his own stunts involving spectacular chase sequences. In addition to three marriages resulting in three children, his private life was marked by numerous affairs and drug abuse.

FREDDIE MERCURY was born as Farrokh Bulsara in 1946 in Zanzibar and died in 1991 in London. Beginning in 1974, this musician of Indian descent became a global star as lead singer and songwriter of the British rock band Queen. Thanks to Mercury's enormous stage presence—a blend of clever costumes, narcissism, and glam rock—Queen became one of the most successful live bands of all time, and he also had success as a solo artist. He died at the age of forty-five of an AIDS-related illness and has since became a legend.

ELVIS PRESLEY was born Elvis Aaron Presley in 1935 in East Tupelo, Mississippi, and died in 1977 in Memphis. He began his career in 1954 as one of the first musicians of the rockabilly movement, a fusion of "white" country and "black" rhythm and blues. He shot to fame in 1956 and became a role model for an entire generation of teenagers. As the "King of Rock 'n' Roll" he went down in music history as the most successful and one of the most popular solo artists of the twentieth century.

PORFIRIO RUBIROSA Ariza was born in 1909 in Santo Domingo, Dominican Republic, the son of a general and diplomat, and died in a car accident in Paris in 1965. He spent most of his youth in Paris, where he later studied. After military service, he became a diplomat in the service of the Dominican Republic, and from the 1930s to 1950s lived in grand style, earning a reputation as a Latin lover. His six marriages were to prominent and wealthy women, and he had affairs with many of the great beauties of the jet set. Apart from women, Rubirosa's greatest passions were fast cars, racing, and polo.

RUN-D.M.C. was a hip-hop group founded in 1982 by Jason Mizell (Jam Master Jay), Joseph Simmons (Run), and Darryl McDaniels (D.M.C.) in Queens, New York. Their first album, released in 1984 and simply titled *Run-D.M.C.*, earned them a gold record, and their subsequent albums went platinum and multi-platinum. Hip-hop pioneers, they were the first rappers featured on the cover of *Rolling Stone* magazine. In 2002 Jam Master Jay was shot and killed by an unknown assailant in a Queens recording studio, signaling the end of Run-D.M.C.

YVES SAINT LAURENT was born in 1936 in Oran, Algeria, and died in 2008 in Paris. Saint Laurent first earned recognition in 1954 when he was awarded the first prize of the International Wool Secretariat. With his first collection for Christian Dior, Ligne Trapèze, he received the world's attention, and with his Op-Art fashions he had a decisive influence on the history of style. After leaving Dior he founded his own fashion label, YSL, with his partner Pierre Bergé. In 1985 he received the highest distinction of the world of fashion, the "Oscar" for lifetime achievement.

THE SEX PISTOLS were from 1975 to 1978 a British punk band composed of Johnny Rotten, Steve Jones, Paul Cook, and Glen Matlock, who was replaced in 1977–78 by Sid Vicious. Apart from the music, it was the Sex Pistols' provocative lyrics and shocking appearance that greatly contributed to the success of punk as a seventies anti-establishment movement. Their album *Never Mind the Bollocks, Here's the Sex Pistols* is seen as a music history milestone and represented the commercial breakthrough of punk music.

FRANK SINATRA was born Francis Albert Sinatra in 1915 in Hoboken, New Jersey, and died in 1998 in Los Angeles. A singer, actor, and entertainer, from the 1940s to the 60s he was a leading show business personality. Earning the nickname "The Voice," his most successful concerts took place in Las Vegas casinos, where he performed in duet with Dean Martin and Sammy Davis Jr., fellow members of the legendary Rat Pack.

HEDI SLIMANE was born in 1968 in Paris. He studied politics and art history at the Ecole du Louvre in Paris. In 1996 he became head designer of Yves Saint Laurent's men's collection, and with his slim cuts and silhouettes made a huge mark on the fashion world. He left the fashion house after three years and is currently active as a fashion designer, artist, and photographer, dividing his time between his homes in Paris and Los Angeles.

ANDRÉ LEON TALLEY was born in 1949 in Durham, North Carolina. While studying French at Brown University he befriended students at the Rhode Island School of Design (RISD) and had his first contact with the world of fashion. In New York he became Diana Vreeland's assistant, and then began his career as a fashion journalist at *Vogue*, for which he still works as a columnist. A popular personality, he has great influence on today's fashion trends.

GIANNI VERSACE was born in 1946 in Calabria, southern Italy, and was shot and killed 1997 in front of his house in Miami. He trained as a tailor in the family business and in 1968 began to work as an independent fashion designer for some of the most renowned Italian fashion houses. In 1979 he founded his own firm, and the eighties witnessed his international breakthrough as a designer. Beginning in 1982 he frequently took on design commissions for theater, opera, and ballet productions.

OSCAR WILDE was born in 1854 in Dublin, Ireland, and died in 1900 in Paris, impoverished and alone. The Irish writer was a leading representative of the aesthetic "art for art's sake" movement. Admired as an author and at the same time decried in Victorian England as a dandy, he consistently criticized the prudery of English society. He was famous for his gilded tongue and flamboyant appearance. In 1884 he married Constance Lloyd, with whom he had two children. His notorious homosexuality, however, offended society, and in 1895 he was sentenced to two years in prison. After his release he lived in Paris until his death under an assumed name.

EDWARD, DUKE OF WINDSOR was born in 1894 in White Lodge, Richmond Park, England, and died in exile in Paris in 1972. He was the Prince of Wales from 1910 to 1936, King Edward VIII of the United Kingdom until his abdication in December 1936, and thereafter the Duke of Windsor. In 1937 he married the divorced American Wallis Simpson, for whom he had given up the throne. They were the first jet-set couple of the postwar years, and were known for their lavish lifestyle and non-stop travel. At the high point of his popularity in the 1920s and 30s, Edward was the world's most photographed person.

TOM WOLFE was born in 1931 in Richmond, Virginia, as Thomas Kennerly Wolfe Jr. He is one of the founders, alongside Truman Capote, of New Journalism, a style of reportage that employs literary techniques in works of non-fiction. After studying at Yale, Wolfe worked as a journalist for the *New York Herald Tribune* and the *Washington Post* among other periodicals. His first novel *The Bonfire of the Vanities*, published in 1987, was a bestseller and secured his international fame. He is considered a cult figure of contemporary literature and lives near New York City on Long Island.

FRONTISPIECE: Mick Jagger poses for a portrait bare-chested and in striped velvet pants, ca. 1969

THE GENTLEMEN

Pierce Brosnan as James Bond with a bow tie and a gun, 1990s; Edward, Duke of Windsor with a pipe in London, 1951; Frank Sinatra wears a hat in the recording studio, 1962; Fred Astaire with a carnation in his buttonhole, 1937; Ralph Lauren in jacket and tie celebrating the 40th anniversary of his company in New York, 2007; John F. Kennedy in a rep tie holding his eyeglasses, 1955; George Clooney in a dark suit and matching shirt at a film premiere in Westwood, 2009

THE REBELS

Steve McQueen in a helmet and goggles at a motorcycle race in the Mojave Desert, 1963; Marlon Brando crossing his arms in a plain t-shirt, ca. 1951; Che Guevara with beret, 1959; Kurt Cobain in a patterned shirt playing his Fender Mustang guitar at Roseland Ballroom, 1993; Johnny Cash in a black shirt at the Country Music Festival, 1980; James Dean on the California set of *East of Eden*, 1954

THE DANDIES

Gianni Agnelli in a business suit, 1970s; Oscar Wilde with carnation and cigarette, 1892; Lapo Elkann in a hat at the Palazzo Grassi, Venice, 2009; Truman Capote wearing glasses in Milan, 1966; Falco wearing a red shirt under a black jacket, undated; Bryan Ferry in a plaid jacket, ca. 1975; Tom Wolfe with a dotted tie and white three-piece suit at home, New York, 1988; André Leon Talley wearing a fur hat in New York, 2010; André Benjamin in a straw hat to receive the Quincy Jones Award, Los Angeles, 2004

THE ROCK STARS

Jimi Hendrix wearing a hat and ring at a Los Angeles press conference, 1968; Freddie Mercury in leather pants and suspenders at a concert in Paris, 1979; Jarvis Cocker in a sports coat at the inaugural Connect Music Festival, Argyll, 2007; Mick Jagger in a stage outfit, Wembley, 1973

THE CLASSICS

Helmut Lang, a self-portrait; Giorgio Armani in a black t-shirt at his gallery opening at the Guggenheim Museum Bilbao, 2001; Hedi Slimane in a striped shirt and pinstripe jacket, Paris, 2007; Marcello Mastroianni smokes a cigarette in a scene from the film *Marriage Italian Style*, 1964

THE FASHION DESIGNERS

Gianni Versace on the cover of his book *Designs*, undated; Yves Saint Laurent with glasses and a cigarette in the office of his Paris studio, 1982; Karl Lagerfeld with silver chains and a tiepin, Paris, 2010; Jean Paul Gaultier in an open white shirt and sports coat at Bergdorf Goodman, 2006; John Galliano poses with a top hat at his Paris fashion show, 2008

THE BEAUTIFUL PEOPLE

Tom Ford with characteristic sunglasses at the International Toronto Film Festival, 2009; Cary Grant in classy threads, 1947; the Carabinieri in uniform, undated; David Beckham in an olive-green knitted cap, Manchester, 2002; Porfirio Rubirosa in a jersey, with a polo pony in Palm Beach, 1955; Johnny Depp in a gray hat and horn-rimmed glasses, Tokyo, 2006

THE BANDS

The Sex Pistols pose in a dumpster, London, 1977; Run-D.M.C. pose in gold chains against the open sky, 1988; the Beatles in black suits at a studio recording, 1962

THE EXTRATERRESTRIALS

Michael Jackson in a gold suit on his *History* tour, Amsterdam, 1997; Ziggy Stardust poses with a dog for his studio album *Diamond Dogs*, London, 1974; Elvis Presley in a sparkling suit at an appearance in Asheville, 1975; Bootsy Collins with floral hat and toy pistol, ca. 1970; Boy George, blond, wearing a red cap, 1987

BIOGRAPHIES

Frank Sinatra in a suit and hat in the recording studio, 1956; James Dean with a red jacket in the film *Rebel Without a Cause*, Los Angeles, 1955; George Clooney in a casual gray suit and open shirt at the Venice Film Festival, 2003; Freddie Mercury in a white bodysuit, ca. 1970; Pierce Brosnan as James Bond, 1990s; Johnny Depp wearing a striped knitted cap at a press conference for the film *Blow*, California, 2001

Cover: James Dean (Michael Ochs Archives/Getty Images), Oscar Wilde (see page 61), Johnny Depp (see page 163), John Galliano (see page 115), Boy George (see page 160), Frank Sinatra (Getty Images)

Frontispiece: Michael Ochs Archives/Getty Images; pages 12/13 l. to r.: Greg Williams/Eon Productions via Getty Images (James Bond); Reg Speller/Fox Photos/Getty Images (Edward Duke of Windsor); Michael Ochs Archives/Getty Images (Frank Sinatra); Ernest Bachrach/John Kobal Foundation/Getty Images (Fred Astaire); Amy Sussman/Getty Images (Ralph Lauren); Verner Reed//Time Life Pictures/Getty Images (John F. Kennedy); Jon Kopaloff/FilmMagic/Getty Images (George Clooney); page 14: Reg Birkett/Keystone/Getty Images; page 15: Popperfoto/Getty Images; page 16: Thomas D. McAvoy/Time & Life Pictures/Getty Images; page 17: William Lovelace/Express/Getty Images; page 18: John Kobal Foundation/Hulton Archive/Getty Images; page 19: Sasha/Getty Images; page 20: Michael Ochs Archive/Getty Images; page 21: Bob Landry/Time Life Pictures/Getty Images; page 23: Metronome/Getty Images; page 24: John Dominis//Time Life Pictures/Getty Images; page 25: Robert Knudsen, White House/John Fitzgerald Kennedy Library, Boston; page 26: Hy Peskin//Time Life Pictures/Getty Images; page 27: AP Photo, File; page 28: Mark Mainz/Getty Images; page 29: Fernanda Calfat/Getty Images for IMG; page 30: M.G.M/UA/EON/Album/AKG; page 31: (large) Michael Ochs Archives/Getty Images; (small) Keystone/Getty Images; page 32: Terrence Spencer//Time Life Pictures/Getty Images; page 33: (large) Terry O'Neill/Getty Images; (small) Greg Williams/Eon Productions via Getty Images; page 34: V. Jackman/FilmMagic/Getty Images; page 35: Pier Giorgio Brunelli/FilmMagic/Getty Images; pages 36/37 l. to r.: John Dominis//Time Life Pictures/Getty Images (Steve McQueen); Hulton Archive/Getty Images (Marlon Brando); Joseph Scherschel//Time Life Pictures/Getty Images (Che Guevara); Ebet Roberts/Redferns/Getty Images (Kurt Cobain); David Redfern/Redferns/Getty Images (Johnny Cash); Michael Ochs Archives/Getty Images (James Dean); page 39: Hulton Archive/Getty Images; page 40: Silver Screen Collection/Hulton Archive/Getty Images; page 41: Ed Clark/Time & Life Pictures/Getty Images; page 43: Alberto Korda by VG Bild Kunst, Bonn 2010; page 44: Silver Screen Collection/Hulton Archive/Getty Images; page 45: (large) Terry O'Neill/Getty Images; (small) Warner Bros./Courtesy Getty Images; page 47: Sunset Boulevard/Corbis; page 48: Hulton Archive/Getty Images; page 49: Michael Ochs Archives/Getty Images; page 51: Michael Ochs Archives/Getty Images; pages 52/53: Central Press/Getty Images; page 54: Kevin Mazur Archive 1/WireImage/Getty Images; page 55: (large) Jeff Kravitz/FilmMagic/Getty Images; (small) Frank Micelotta/Getty Images; pages 56/57 l. to r.: Authenticated News/Getty Images (Gianni Agnelli); Ellis&Walery, London (Oscar Wilde); Vittorio Zunino Celotto/Getty Images (Lapo Elkann); Keystone/Getty Images (Truman Capote); AP Photo/ho (Falco); Michael Ochs Archives/Getty Images (Brian Ferry); Ulf Andersen/Getty Images (Tom Wolfe); Gary Gershoff/WireImage/Getty Images (André Leon Talley); Carlo Allegri/Getty Images (André Benjamin); page 58: Jabez, Hughes & Mullins; page 59: Napoleon Sarony; page 60: Napoleon Sarony; page 61: Napoleon Sarony; page 62: David Lees/Time Life Pictures/Getty Images; page 63: David Lees/Time Life Pictures/Getty Images; page 65: Jerry Cooke/Time & Life Pictures/Getty Images; page 66: Library Of Congress/Hulton Archive/Getty

Images; page 67: CBS Photo Archive/Getty Images; page 68: Dimitrios Kambouris/WireImage for Rubenstein Communications, Inc./Getty Images; page 69: Martha Holmes/Time & Life Pictures/Getty Images; (small above) Jorgen Angel/Redferns/Getty Images; (small below) Gijsbert Hanekroot/Redferns/Getty Images; page 72: Elisabetta Villa/Getty Images; page 73: (large) Stephen Lovekin/WireImage for Nathan Jensen/Getty Images; (small) Slaven Vlasic/Getty Images; page 75: www.starsandpictures.com/Curt Themessl; page 76: John Rogers/Getty Images; page 77: Jim Spellman/WireImage/Getty Images; page 78: Venturelli/WireImage/Getty Images; page 79: Franco Origlia/Getty Images; pages 80/81 l. to r.: Michael Ochs Archives/Getty Images (Jimi Hendrix); Georges DeKeerle/Getty Images (Freddie Mercury); Jim Dyson/Getty Images (Jarvis Cocker); David Redfern/Redferns/Getty Images (Mick Jagger); page 82: David Redfern/Redferns/Getty Images; page 83: Terence Donovan Archive/Getty Images; page 84: Debi Doss/Hulton Archive/Getty Images; page 85: David Drapkin/Getty Images; page 86: Suzie Gibbons/Redferns/Getty Images; page 87: (large) Michael Ochs Archives/Getty Images; (small above) Waring Abbott/Getty Images; (small below) Paul Natkin/WireImage/Getty Images; page 88: Eamonn McCabe/Redferns/Getty Images; page 89: Tony Buckingham/Redferns/Getty Images; pages 90/91 l. to r.: Helmut Lang (Self portrait, 2007) (Helmut Lang); Christophe Simon/AFP/Getty Images (Giorgio Armani); Eric Ryan/Getty Images (Hedi Slimane); Alfred Eisenstaedt//Time Life Pictures/Getty Images (Marcello Mastroianni); page 93: Hulton Archive/Getty Images; page 95: Dave Benett/Getty Images; page 97: Mark Von Holden/FilmMagic/Getty Images; page 98: Miguel Villagran/Stringer/Getty Images; page 99: Emmanuel Fradin/Reuters/Corbis; pages 100/101 l. to r.: Ron Galella/WireImage/Getty Images (Gianni Versace); John Downing/Getty Images (Yves Saint Laurent); Foc Kan/WireImage/Getty Images (Karl Lagerfeld); Rabbani and Solimene Photography/WireImage/Getty Images (Jean Paul Gaultier); Eric Ryan/Getty Images (John Galliano); page 102: Antonio de Moraes Barros Filho/WireImage/Getty Images; page 103: (large) Vittorio Zunino Celotto/Getty Images; (small) Venturelli/WireImage/Getty Images; page 105: YSL Yves Saint Laurent/Jeanloup Sieff/Image courtesy of The Advertising Archives; page 107: Toni Thorimbert/Sygma/Corbis; pages 108/109: Vittoriano Rastelli/Corbis; page 110: Ron Galella, Ltd./WireImage/Getty Images; page 111: Julien Hekimian/Getty Images; page 113: Maison Martin Margiela; page 114: Brian Ach/WireImage/Getty Images; page 115: Karl Prouse/Catwalking/Getty Images; pages 116/117 l. to r.: Matt Carr/Getty Images (Tom Ford); John Kobal Foundation/Getty Images (Cary Grant); Tommaso Montenegro – wSphoto (Carabinieri); John Peters/Manchester United via Getty Images (David Beckham); Morgan Collection/Getty Images (Porfirio Rubirosa); Yuji Ohsugi/WireImage/Getty Images (Johnny Depp); page 118: Paolo Di Paolo/Silvana Editorale; page 119: (large) Brian Trosko; (small) Paolo Di Paolo/Silvana Editorale; page 120: Paolo Di Paolo/Silvana Editorale; page 121: Paolo Di Paolo/Silvana Editorale; page 122: Hulton Archive/Getty Images; page 123: John Kobal Foundation/Getty Images; page 124: Silver Screen Collection/Getty Images; page 125: Keystone/Hulton Archive/Getty Images; page 126: Morgan Collection/Getty Images; page 127: (small) Thurston Hopkins/Getty Images; (large) Picture Post/Getty